CLOAK-AND-DAGGER BIBLIOGRAPHY

An Annotated Guide to Spy Fiction,

1937-1975

by

MYRON J. SMITH, Jr.

The Scarecrow Press, Inc.

Metuchen, N.J.   1976

"I only regret that I have but one life to lose for my country."
 --Nathan Hale, 22 September 1776

Library of Congress Cataloging in Publication Data

Smith, Myron J
    Cloak-and-dagger bibliography.

    Includes index.
    1. Spy stories, English--20th century--Bibliog-
raphy. 2. Spy stories, American--20th century--
Bibliography. 3. English fiction--20th century--
Stories, plots, etc. 4. American fiction--20th
century--Stories, plots, etc. I. Title.
Z2014.F5S62 [PR830.S65] 016.823'0872   75-44319
ISBN 0-8108-0897-8

for

Karen and Jim

INTRODUCTION

Secret agents, meaning basically spies, saboteurs, and commando-style operatives, have been around for thousands of years. Their activities in behalf of church, state, business, or other groups probably began in those dim distant days when Homo sapiens first began organizing to "liquidate" their predecessors and ice covered huge portions of the earth. Certainly these people were well known in ancient Israel; the Old Testament reveals that Joshua and Moses led an all-star cast of agents. A little further north and a bit later in time, boy-wonder Alexander the Great and Julius Caesar both profited handsomely from their rather efficient espionage apparatuses. This trend continued right on up through Daniel Defoe, who more or less started British Intelligence; Nathan Hale, who set a prime example for Americans; Mrs. Rose O. Greenhow who spied the Yankees into disaster at Bull Run; Mata Hari who blew it during World War I; Allan Dulles and Dusko Popov who performed wonders during World War II; and E. Howard Hunt who is still in the daily news.

The business of these people and thousands like them over the last several millenia has been intelligence-gathering and clandestine operations. Napoleon once remarked that a spy in the right place was worth an extra 20,000 men in the field. In short, these brave souls have usually been charged with obtaining something (information) or busting up something (secret installations) in the homeland or conquered territory of a particular enemy. This idea was well put in a 10 September 1775 letter by Nathan Hale: "Every kind of service [i.e., espionage, clandestine operations] necessary to the public good, becomes honorable by being necessary."

Naturally the kinds of things we have been talking about were not and are not done "in the open," but secretly, under cover. Men and women have worked individually in such pursuits or in groups, such as those organized in occupied Europe during the Second World War. This sort of activity, prior to the invention of spy satellites and electronic gear, has always been dangerous. Its operatives have historically been beyond the honor code and the regular rules of war pertaining to uniformed combatants. Every agent has always known that being unmasked is most likely fatal.

What kind of people take up this sort of profession and what keeps them at it? Writing in his The Art of War, Sun Tzu (400-320 B.C.) summed up the best type of operative in advice which has usually been followed ever since:

> As living spies we must recruit men [and now women] who are intelligent, but appear to be stupid; who seem to be dull, but are strong in heart; men who are agile, vigorous, hardy, and brave; well-versed in lowly matters and able to endure hunger, cold, filth, and humiliation.

Motives for being a secret agent have doubtless ranged from money to vengeance for particular wrongs to the idea of making mankind safe for a particular ideology. Public glory has not been a drawing card primarily because of the hush-hush aspect of the business.

The life of a spy, as opposed to the commando-saboteur, can be a very lonely and dull affair. Unlike the fictional concept which we will discuss in a moment, most real-life operatives are cogs in efficient machines run from afar, a fact which has been true for centuries. The necessity of order and routine does not leave much room for the James Bonds in everyday espionage or even in clandestine operations. This is not to say that these people have never existed; only that they have not been as numerous as a thriller-reader might expect.

There will always be a need for espionage and secret operations as long as there is tension or war in the world. The days of the human secret agent gathering data behind enemy lines may, as some claim, be on the way out in the face of electronic or satellite technology, but one must suspect that the need for this sort of service and especially for the commando-style specialist will continue to be a necessity for a good many years yet to come.

Despite the historical presence of secret agents, the fictional literature of their exploits has been primarily a 20th-century phenomenon (and basically a British one at that). This is true probably because for thousands of years writers, philosophers, and military people in general simply did not like to admit that such creatures existed or were beneficial to the aims of "great" nations. Much of this changed in light of the monumental scandal in France late last century known as "The Dreyfus Affair," and continued right on through to World War I and the years beyond. The influx of undercover memoirs produced after World War II also undoubtedly contributed to the public knowledge of such activities. *

Once the idea of secret operatives was thus established in the public eye, serious writers began to turn their attention to developing what would eventually become a spy-adventure mania. The first spy story as we know it in light of present fiction was probably Erskine Childers' The Riddle of the Sands, published in Britain in 1900. † The first major writer to deal with the topic was Joseph Conrad in his The Secret Agent, another British effort, in 1907. After Conrad came such early giants as William Le Queux, E. Phillips Oppenheim, and John Buchan.

Although spy-adventure stories have long been widely read in America, it was not until comparatively recently that Yankee writers penned very many of them. The first important American to author the type of story we have been discussing was John P. Marquand, whose Mr. Moto series was published in the 1930's. During the James Bond era there were many more, especially in the paperback field.

As the literature of secret agents developed, it began to overlap with detective, suspense, and intrigue adventure. People like Eric Ambler, Helen MacInnes, and Graham Greene entered the lists, writing stories in which operatives were involved but not vital to main themes or in which unofficial agents (journalists, scientists, et al.) were recruited to investigate sundry goings-on. And of course espionage sometimes caused murders which needed to be solved by daring private eyes of Scotland Yard or the gumshoes of the L. A. P. D.

Besides reminiscences of true-life capers, World War II brought a raft of secret-agent adventures to fiction and for the first time the introduction of tales which specialized in

---

*See George Siehl, "Cloak, Dust Jacket, and Dagger," Library Journal 97 (Oct. 15, 1972), 3277-3283.
†James F. Cooper's The Spy concerns Loyalists not agents during the Revolution; Alexander Dumas' character Milady is only incidental to the tale of The Three Musketeers.

clandestine operations, i.e., small guerrilla or commando bands doing in the Axis enemy or his projects. This time span has been a fertile backdrop for spy-adventure for almost thirty years now, with Alistair MacLean and Colin Forbes the undisputed masters of group mischief.

The period of the Cold War probably did more than anything to get the spy-adventure off the ground and turn it into a literary cult by the middle 1960's. The proliferation of small wars of independence, the stalemate among big powers created by the A-bomb and tension over its possible use and secrets, such mind-boggling episodes as the McCarthy ravings, the U-2 Incident, and the Bay of Pigs all cried out for relief. This relief was provided the average citizen, when he was not out digging bomb shelters, in the gutsy secret agent tale of the James Bond era.

During the period from say 1954 (when Fleming published his first 007 adventure, Casino Royale) until about 1971, when the genre began to recede, the super-agent spy story was in vogue everywhere in the Western world and to a limited extent, even in Warsaw-Pact nations. No longer were operatives the dull real-life types described earlier (with the exception of those created by John le Carré and a few of his followers), but deadly amourous amoral falcons of good who always triumphed over often grisly, sometimes humorous obstacles presented by a multitude of mad villains. No longer was "the enemy" always Russia or China; sometimes it was a conglomerate of super-national criminals out to do in all governments and control the world. T.H.R.U.S.H. of the popular American TV series, "The Man from Uncle," was such a group. Beautiful women, sex, and sadism (not to mention deadly and strange weapons and general mayhem) became the props of good and bad guys alike: those choosing or reading such material should keep this fact in mind.

Television and advertising proved a big supporter of the frenzy, with viewers entertained night after night with the destruction of various nasties by "The Secret Agent," "The Avengers," and "U.N.C.L.E." (man and girl from), and on such other shows as "I Spy," "Mission Impossible," and even "Get Smart," to name a few. Commercials during those programs often represented the theme, complete to the briefly-clad girl and the unwholesome villain.

Movies also contributed to the craze and throughout the period this book covers were delivered up wholesale until the market was glutted and theater-goers began to pass them up. *

    While authors continue to turn out spy-adventure tales,
now often concerning petro-politics and various terrorist
groups, the big Bond boom is quite past. This is true, I
suspect, for two important reasons and perhaps several others. First, rising from humble beginnings, the spy-adventure became a fad like the Western and after awhile, like
the horse opera, it began to be replaced by new themes, one
of which was organized crime and the effort of various police
organizations to halt it; or, putting it another way, the revival of the more-ancient mystery story with new slants.
One suspects that this theme will one day be replaced, but
by what is anyone's guess. Science Fiction? Sea Stories?

    Secondly, at least in America, disillusionment with
war and revelations of gross governmental immorality have
soured the public. For the better part of a decade, we had
gloried in the fiction and escapism of clandestinism, but now
we are horrified to discover that, in reality, much of it was
practiced against segments of the U.S. public. If you spend
very much time reading the sort of literature I cite in this
Bibliography, you cannot but come to the conclusion that the
C.I.A., a statutory <u>overseas</u> intelligence agency, has been
very much involved <u>within the</u> borders of the United States
on a regular basis. However in fairness to "the company, "
I must point out that the <u>fiction</u> herein listed <u>must</u> <u>not</u> be
used as the basis for an <u>opinion</u> concerning <u>possible illegal</u>
acts for which that organization came under investigation in
early 1975. It is always important to separate the spy groups
of fiction from the spy groups of real life and to do that, I
strongly recommend that you read whatever official information and secondary works (books, magazine articles, news-
papers) that are available for research. And even there you
must carefully weigh the exposé against the objective analysis.

    Despite what I have been saying here about the causes
behind the rise and fall of the spy-adventure, there remains
a good audience of fans anxious to peruse the literature.
This fact is daily brought home to me in my capacity as a
public librarian and I am told it is evident in secondary
schools as well. The need for a tool such as this one exists

---

*For 463 of these, complete with detailed credits and plot
summaries plus 150 photos, see James R. Parish and Michael R. Pitts, <u>The Great Spy Pictures</u> (Metuchen, N.J.:
Scarecrow Press, 1974).

and now after most of the cloaks-and-daggers have been hung in the closet, the time is ripe for its presentation.

About the Bibliography

This book is an alphabetically-arranged volume of selected spy-adventure-intrigue novels written between the years 1937 and mid-1975. I had as my main goal in compiling it the choosing of titles of interest to the adult and young-adult (high-school) reader and that are representative especially of the World War II and James Bond eras.

Just as I selected the over 1600 titles for cross-section representativeness, so too did I carefully consider the annotations. It was a difficult task to decide in a very short space how much of a book's flavor could be revealed; nevertheless, the majority of these notes reveal something of the plot, characters, or special aspects making volumes unique. In reading these, you will quickly discover, as I did, that many themes repeat themselves from book to book or author to author, usually with different twists. I offer these as content citations only; the individual reader must determine for himself which tales are "best" to his own way of thinking.

In some cases, I felt that it would be a greater service to annotate one, two, or a few more of an author's works and then simply list others. Thus you will occasionally find two or more title entries at the end of an author's listings that are out of alphabetical order, reflecting this purposeful annotation-first policy. This selected annotation effort has been employed primarily in the case of writers who have written many titles using either the same character or similar plots. Examples are Edward S. Aarons, Simon Harvester, Nick Carter, Donald Hamilton, etc. By and large, however, all titles are annotated, as described above.

Readers' Tastes

A special problem exists for the spy-adventure reader in the area of the male-oriented exclusively paperback action series. I have entered a number of these, but they are currently being produced so rapidly (in some cases two per quarter) that you will have to check your Forthcoming Books or visit your bookshop to keep up. If you elect the latter, be sure to check titles carefully, as publishers of this material change the design of their dustjackets with each reissuance.

Each of the titles herein is given a serial entry number, to which numbers in the Title Index refer. Additionally, the symbol "P" has been employed to indicate those books available exclusively in softbound editions. I have also employed three other symbols which are deserving of your attention.

In my opinion, very little of this spy-adventure fiction is suitable for young readers, especially those below the tenth grade. On the other hand, such standards as Ian Fleming's works do appear in high school library collections. To help you determine titles of possible use for less-than-tenth-grade readers, I have added the symbol "Y" after those titles that may be serviceable. These should perhaps be checked for local standards of taste, etc., before handing out. Likewise, as was mentioned above, sex, sadism, violence, and general mayhem are, for the most part, features of this genre and are present in some degree in every title cited herein. As a help when you might need to choose titles where the sex level, at least, is low, the symbol "*" is added after those entries where this is the case. The symbol "H" refers to titles of a humorous bent, both "ho ho" and satirical. To summarize the symbols:

P exclusively in paper-   * sex level lower than
   back   most

Y more suitable than   H humor a major feature
   most for under-
   10th-graders

An effort has also been made to separate writers' pen-names from real names and where successful, titles are entered under the latter. Cross references are made from pseudonyms to writers.

In 1640, George Herbert wrote in his Outlandish Proverbs: "The life of spies is to know, not to be known." It is to be hoped that this present exercise will help to unlock for you what in fiction these past thirty-odd years has been the exact opposite of that ancient adage.

Myron J. Smith, Jr.
Huntington, Indiana
November 1975

THE BIBLIOGRAPHY

1 Aarons, Edward S. Assignment: Amazon Queen. Greenwich, Conn.: Fawcett, 1974. P
   A goodly number of titles have been published in this exclusively paperback series on daring CIA agent Sam Durell. In this particular yarn, he is sent to South America to uncover a Nazi plot and becomes involved, as always, with a beautiful girl. Other titles in the series--one of the best softbound ones--follow.

2 _____. Assignment: Andalusa. Greenwich, Conn.: Fawcett, 1965. P

3 _____. Assignment: Angelina. Greenwich, Conn.: Fawcett, 1958. P
   Her name meant "Little Angel," but she was an enemy agent.

4 _____. Assignment: Ankara. Greenwich, Conn.: Fawcett, 1969. P
   A dangerous mission to Turkey.

5 _____. Assignment: Argentina. Greenwich, Conn.: Fawcett, 1964. P

6 _____. Assignment: Bangkok. Greenwich, Conn.: Fawcett, 1972. P

7 _____. Assignment: Black Viking. Greenwich, Conn.: Fawcett, 1972. P

8 _____. Assignment: Budapest. Greenwich, Conn.: Fawcett, 1974. P

9 _____. Assignment: Burma Girl. Greenwich, Conn.: Fawcett, 1973. P

10 _____. Assignment: The Cairo Dancers. Greenwich, Conn.: Fawcett, 1974. P
   A secret underground railway of espionage.

11 _____. Assignment: Carlotta Cortez. Greenwich, Conn.: Fawcett, 1972. P

12 _____. Assignment: Ceylon. Greenwich, Conn.:
Fawcett, 1973. P
Durell chases a defecting diplomat, kisses a beautiful Singhalese politician, and is menaced by a "messenger of evil."

13 _____. Assignment: Cong Hai Kill. Greenwich,
Conn.: Fawcett, 1973. P

14 _____. Assignment: Girl in the Gondola. Greenwich,
Conn.: Fawcett, 1974. P

15 _____. Assignment: Golden Girl. Greenwich, Conn.:
Fawcett, 1972. P

16 _____. Assignment: Helene. Greenwich, Conn.:
Fawcett, 1959. P

17 _____. Assignment: Karachi. Greenwich, Conn.:
Fawcett, 1973. P
Millionaire businesswoman in the Himalayas.

18 _____. Assignment: Lili Lamaris. Greenwich, Conn.:
Fawcett, 1973. P

19 _____. Assignment: London. Greenwich, Conn.:
Fawcett, 1963. P

20 _____. Assignment: Lowlands. Greenwich, Conn.:
Fawcett, 1961. P
Notes keep coming in about a catastrophe. Then Durell is sent to Holland to find Cassandra in 47 hours.

21 _____. Assignment: Madeleine. Greenwich, Conn.:
Fawcett, 1971. P

22 _____. Assignment: Malta. Greenwich, Conn.:
Fawcett, 1966. P

23 _____. Assignment: Maltese Maiden. Greenwich,
Conn.: Fawcett, 1972. P

24 _____. Assignment: Manchurian Doll. Greenwich,
Conn.: Fawcett, 1972. P

25 _____. Assignment: Mara Tirana. Greenwich, Conn.:
Fawcett, 1972. P

26 _____. Assignment: Moon Girl. Greenwich, Conn.:
Fawcett, 1972. P

27 _____. Assignment: New York. Greenwich, Conn.:
Fawcett, 1963. P

28 _____. Assignment: Nuclear Nude. Greenwich,

Conn.:   Fawcett, 1973.   P

29 _____.   Assignment: Palermo.   Greenwich, Conn.:
Fawcett, 1972.   P

30 _____.   Assignment: Peking.   Greenwich, Conn.:
Fawcett, 1972.   P
Durell made up like a Chinaman, is sent to the
mainland.

31 _____.   Assignment: Quayle Question.   Greenwich,
Conn.:   Fawcett, 1975.   P
Face-to-face with a madman who wants to rule
the world.

32 _____.   Assignment: School for Spies.   Greenwich,
Conn.:   Fawcett, 1970.   P

33 _____.   Assignment: Sea Bird.   Greenwich, Conn.:
Fawcett, 1969.   P

34 _____.   Assignment: Silver Scorpion.   Greenwich,
Conn.:   Fawcett, 1973.   P

35 _____.   Assignment: Sorrento Siren.   Greenwich,
Conn.:   Fawcett, 1973.   P

36 _____.   Assignment: Star Stealers.   Greenwich,
Conn.:   Fawcett, 1972.   P

37 _____.   Assignment: Stella Marni.   Greenwich,
Conn.:   Fawcett, 1974.   P

38 _____.   Assignment: Suicide.   Greenwich, Conn.:
Fawcett, 1972.   P

39 _____.   Assignment: Sulu Sea.   Greenwich, Conn.:
Fawcett, 1964.   P
Atomic submarine vanishes.

40 _____.   Assignment: Sumatra.   Greenwich, Conn.:
Fawcett, 1974.   P

41 _____.   Assignment: To Disaster.   Greenwich, Conn.:
Fawcett, 1972.   P

42 _____.   Assignment: Tokyo.   Greenwich, Conn.:
Fawcett, 1971.   P

43 _____.   Assignment: Treason.   Greenwich, Conn.:
Fawcett, 1973.   P

44 _____.   Assignment: White Rajah.   Greenwich, Conn.:
Fawcett, 1974.   P
American fighter planes hijacked in Southeast Asia.

45 _____. Assignment: Zoraya. Greenwich, Conn. :
Fawcett, 1972. P

Addeo, Edmond G., coauthor see Garvin, Richard M.

45a Albert, Marvin. The Gargoyle Conspiracy. Garden City,
N. Y. : Doubleday, 1975.
An agent must locate and eliminate an Arab terrorist
group plotting the assassination of the U. S. Secretary of
State.

Albrand, Martha, pseud. see Loewengard, Heidi H.

Aldanov, Mark, pseud. see Landau, Mark A.

46 Aldridge, James. A Captive in the Land. Garden City,
N. Y. : Doubleday, 1963. *
Englishman Royce saves an injured Russian in the
Arctic, is invited to Soviet Union for a medal; there
he is tailed by British and American agents, but unbeknownst to them is on a spying mission for the Royal Navy.

47 _____. The Statesman's Game. Garden City, N. Y.:
Doubleday, 1966. *
Royce once more deals with the Soviets, trading
British ships for Russian oil; Naval Intelligence
quashes that and Royce turns to the Chinese.

48 Allbeury, Ted. Snowball. Philadelphia: Lippincott,
1974. *
The Reds have a document showing that America
and Canada once planned to abandon Great Britain to
Hitler; British agent is assigned to retrieve that paper
before its contents can be leaked to the world.

49 Allingham, Margery. Pearls Before Swine. Garden
City, N. Y. : Doubleday, 1945. Y*
Art treasures, artificial pearls, and a champion
sow are linked in a mystery of crime and espionage.

50 Ambler, Eric. Background to Danger. New York:
Knopf, 1937. *
First published in England as Uncommon Danger.
An agent ordered to Turkey to help keep that country
out of the Axis meets Russian woman defector who
gives him secret papers about a Soviet invasion of
Turkey. She is liquidated and German and Russians
begin chasing agent.

51 _____. Cause for Alarm. New York: Knopf, 1938. *
Quiet young English engineer, as manager of the
Spartacus Machine Tool Co. in Milan, puts a kink in
the Rome-Berlin Axis.

52 _____. A Coffin for Dimitrios. New York: Knopf,
1939. *
First published in England as The Mask of Dimitrios. English writer tracks down the life story of
international intrigue of a nondescript Greek fig-packer
who turns up in a Turkish morgue.

53 _____. Dirty Story. New York: Atheneum, 1968. *
Arthur Simpson attempts to flee Greece and ends
up joining a mercenary army hired to fight in Africa.

54 _____. Doctor Frigo. New York: Atheneum, 1974. *
Espionage and intrigue in Central America; a con-
sortium of big countries out to reap huge profits and
spill blood.

55 _____. Epitaph for a Spy. New York: Knopf, 1952. *
Timid language teacher visiting Nice is arrested as
a spy and is used by British Naval Intelligence.

56 _____. The Intercom Conspiracy. New York:
Atheneum, 1969. *
Two intelligence agents from small N.A.T.O.
countries use secret information to embarrass America
and Russia.

57 _____. Intrigue: Four Great Spy Novels. New York:
Knopf, 1960. *
Three of the four novels contained herein are cited;
see entries 50, 52, and 59.

58. _____. The Intriguers: Four Superb Novels of Suspense. New York: Knopf, 1965. *
Contains Judgment on Deltchev, Passage of Arms,
The Schirmer Inheritance, and State of Siege (all
which see).

59 _____. Journey into Fear. New York: Knopf, 1940. *
German agents pursue an English engineer returning with intelligence from neutral Italy.

60 _____. Judgment on Deltchev. New York: Knopf,
1951. *

An English playwright reports a trial from inside
a Communist country; becomes involved in Cold War
intrigue.

61 _____. A Kind of Anger. New York: Atheneum,
    1964. *
         Piet Maas, something less than an ace reporter,
    is sent on a shot assignment: find the beautiful,
    bikini-clad witness to the murder of an Iraqui politi-
    cian.

62 _____. The Levanter. New York: Atheneum,
    1972. *
         A radical breakaway group of Palestinian terrorists
    plans to wreak havoc in Tel Aviv.

63 _____. The Light of Day. New York: Knopf, 1962. *
         Arthur Simpson, small-time thief, is drawn into a
    conspiracy plotting the world's most daring crime.

64 _____. Passage of Arms. New York: Knopf, 1959. *
         An Indian clerk, two Chinese brothers, and a mid-
    dle-aged American couple in a plot to smuggle arms
    to anti-Communist forces in Indonesia.

65 _____. The Schirmer Inheritance. New York: Knopf,
    1953. *
         A lawyer searches for the lost heir to an Ameri-
    can fortune among the displaced peoples of post-war
    Europe.

66 _____. State of Siege. New York: Knopf, 1956. *
         First published in England as The Night Comes.
    Two English civilians caught in the crossfire in an at-
    tack on a Southeast Asian capital.

67 _____, ed. To Catch a Spy: An Anthology of Favour-
    ite Spy Stories. New York: Atheneum, 1965. *
         By various leading spy writers; note especially
    Ambler's introduction, which contains the best discus-
    sion I have seen on the spy story as a genre.

68 _____, and Charles Rodda. Tender to Danger. By
    Eliot Read, pseud. Garden City, N.Y.: Doubleday,
    1952.
         A vacationing Scot is convinced that something
    sinister is about to happen in Belgium. Rebuffed by

the Belgian police, he returns to England where he
finds he was right.

69 Amis, Kingsley. The Anti-Death League. New York:
Harcourt, 1966.
Preparations for "Operation Apollo," destined to
inflict death in a grisly manner on randomly selected
Red Chinese.

70 _____. Colonel Sun. By Robert Markham, pseud.
New York: Harper, 1968.
Sequel to Ian Fleming's James Bond series; "M"
is captured by Colonel Sun of the People's Liberation
Army of China and held prisoner in Greece. Bond to
the rescue.

71 Anderson, James. The Alpha List. New York: Walker,
1973.
Agents must locate the persons listed.

72 _____. Assassin. New York: Simon & Schuster,
1970.
Awaiting execution in a Middle Eastern jail, our
"hero" is offered his freedom if he will kill a head of
state. To insure his success, the nasties give him
an injection which will kill him in three months unless
he returns for the antidote.

73 Annesley, Michael. Agent Intervenes. London: Paul,
1944. *
Agents look into a Nazi scheme which could prove
immensely embarrassing to the Allied offensive.

74 _____. Spies Abounding. London: Paul, 1945. *
The English intelligence system in World War II.

75 _____. Spies Against the Reich. London: Paul,
1940. *
Early wartime story: Britain, back to the wall,
is well served by heroic spies who steal into the
Reich, steal secrets, and steal back with them to
Britain. Here are some additional classic spy stories
by this excellent contemporary British master.

76 _____. Spy Corner. London: Paul, 1948. *

77 _____. Spy Counter-Spy. London: Paul, 1948. *

78 _____. Spy Island. London: Paul, 1950. *

79 _____. Suicide Spies. London: Paul, 1944. *

80 _____. They Won't Lie Down. London: Paul, 1947. *

81 _____. Unknown Agent. London: Paul, 1940. *

82 _____. The Vanished Vice Counsul. London: Paul,
        1939. *

83 Anthony, Evelyn. The Legend. New York: Coward-
     McCann, 1969. *
     A retired British spy attends a weekend party,
     meets a beautiful divorcee, and ... back in the busi-
     ness.

84 _____. Mission to Malaspiga. New York: Coward-
     McCann, 1974. *
     Italian relatives are suspected of smuggling heroin
     into America via their export trade.

85 _____. The Poellenberg Inheritance. New York:
     Coward-McCann, 1972.
     Paula Stanley's father, an ex-SS general long
     thought dead, informs her through an intermediary that
     a priceless Cellini "stolen" from him is available.
     Others, willing to murder, want it again.

86 _____. Stranger at the Gate. New York: Coward-
     McCann, 1973.
     A banker on business from Switzerland in German-
     occupied France during the war is in fact an American
     O. S. S. officer.

87 _____. The Tamarind Seed. New York: Coward-
     McCann, 1971.
     American Judith Farrow flies to Barbados and
     romance with a Soviet U.N. diplomat (and spy). An
     international crisis develops as each is suspected of
     defecting.

88 Appleby, John. Secret Mountains. New York: Washburn,
     1957.
     Intrigue in the tiny country of Andorra high in the
     Pyrenees.

89 Ardies, Tom. Kosygin Is Coming. Garden City, N.Y.:
     Doubleday, 1974. *
     Before the Soviet premier will visit Vancouver, a
     Latvian fanatic must be taken out of circulation. A

brash lower-rung intelligence agent is given the job of
kidnapping him.

90 _____. This Suitcase Is Going to Explode. Garden
City, N.Y.: Doubleday, 1973. *
Atomic bombs have been hidden around the country
in suitcases in a massive blackmail plot. Washington-
based A.S.P.I.R.E. must hunt them down.

90a Ardman, Harvey. Endgame. New York: Avon, 1975.
Three men and a woman fight for their lives and
nations amongst Arab oil, atomic secrets, and counterespionage.

91 Arent, Arthur. Gravedigger's Funeral. New York:
Grossman, 1967. *
American playwright is off to Germany to find an
older brother. A neo-Nazi group there does not want
him to succeed.

92 _____. The Laying on of Hands. Boston: Little,
Brown, 1970.
Fergus John and a friend set out to locate his
parents and run smack into Israeli agents hunting a
former Nazi concentration camp doctor. Flying on to
Vienna from New York, they learn about ODESSA (that
undercover batch of ex-SS nasties which Frederick
Forsyth writes so well about in The Odessa File--q.v.).

Armstrong, Anthony, pseud. see Willis, Anthony A.

93 Arnold, Elliott. The Commandos. New York: Duell,
1942. *
Training and deployment of British clandestine
military groups against German-occupied Norway.

94 _____. Code of Conduct. New York: Scribner's,
1970.
NAS intelligence officer in Switzerland for another
view of the Pueblo incident.

95 Arvay, Harry. Operation Kuwait. New York: Bantam,
1975. P.
Introduces a new paperback team from the Israeli
Security Branch which here attempts to breakup a
terrorist skyjack training encampment in the desert.

95a   . The Piraeus Plot. New York: Bantam,
      1975. P
          Israeli intelligence agents work to foil a plot
      against Yasser Arafat.

96   Ash, William. Ride a Paper Tiger. New York:
      Walker, 1969.
          Kyle Brandeis flees to a small South African
      nation; espionage and guerrillas.

97   Atkinson, Hugh. The Man in the Middle. New York:
      Putnam, 1973. *
          Penniless interpreter against the oil interests
      of Russia and the Arabs: when he translates secret
      documents he can no longer be permitted to live.

98   Atlee, Philip. The Kowloon Contract. New York:
      Pinnacle Books, 1974. P
          Freelance superspy Joe Gall, top-secret nulli-
      fier, America's ace hit man, bounces around the
      Far East investigating Communists, dispatching
      nasties, and eventually leveling eight acres in the
      middle of a city. Additional titles in the exclusively
      paperback Joe Gall Contract series include:

99   . The Black Venus Contract. New York:
      Pennacle Books, 1975. P

100   . The Canadian Bomber Contract. New
      York: Pinnacle Books, 1971. P

100a   . The Death Bird Contract. New York:
      Pinnacle Books, 1966. P
          Must locate a shady U.S. diplomat in Mexico.

101   . The Fer-de-Lance Contract. New York:
      Pinnacle Books, 1973. P

102   . The Ill Wind Contract. New York: Pin-
      nacle Books, 1971. P
          Must remove five tons of gold from rebel camp
      in war-torn Indonesia.

103   . The Irish Beauty Contract. New York:
      Pinnacle Books, 1972. P

104   . The Judah Lion Contract. New York:
      Pinnacle Books, 1972. P

105   . The Kiwi Contract. New York: Pinnacle
      Books, 1974. P

Gall masquerades as a millionaire marked for murder.

106 _____. The Paper Pistol Contract. New York: Pinnacle Books, 1971. P

107 _____. The Rockabye Contract. New York: Pinnacle Books, 1973. P

108 _____. The Shankill Road Contract. New York: Pinnacle Books, 1974. P

109 _____. The Silken Baroness Contract. New York, 1973. P

110 _____. The Spice Route Contract. New York: Pinnacle Books, 1973. P

111 _____. The Star Ruby Contract. New York: Pinnacle Books, 1973. P
In Burma; Gall gets help from an entire Gurkha regiment.

111a _____. The Trembling Earth Contract. New York: Pinnacle Books, 1969. P
Gall masquerades as a soul brother to halt a militant Black uprising.

112 _____. The Underground Cities Contract. New York: Pinnacle Books, 1974. P
Double-dealing Turkish terrorists.

August, John, pseud. see DeVoto, Bernard A.

113 Avallon, Michael. Assassins Don't Die in Bed. New York: Signet, 1968. P
Ed Noon, former private detective, takes role as "private spy" to the President and plays red herring to a killer. This Noon series reads much better than the Lanny Budd series by Upton Sinclair cited below.

114 _____. The Birds of a Feather Affair. New York: Signet, 1966. PH
Part of the craze over the TV spy series; this story introduces readers to April Dancer, the "Girl from U.N.C.L.E.," who must rescue a fellow agent captured by T.H.R.U.S.H.

115 _____. A Blazing Affair. New York: Signet, 1966. PH

April travels from Budapest to Johannesburg on
the trail of a Fourth Reich organization dedicated
to building a super-race.

116   _____. The Doomsday Bag. New York: Signet,
1969. P
The "bagman" was the man who accompanied
the President with a satchel filled with nuclear-
attack codes. One day he turns up missing, and
Ed Noon is commissioned by the President to get
him and them back--fast!

117   _____. The February Doll Murders. New York:
Signet, 1968. P
Agent Noon tackles a Communist spy ring with
an ingenious plot to sabotage the U.N.

118   _____. Missing. New York: Signet, 1969. P
President-elect is missing and Ed Noon is selected by the current White House occupant to find
him.

          _____ see also Holly, J. Hunter

119   Ayer, Frederick. The Man in the Mirror. Chicago:
Regnery, 1965. *
The President's Special Assistant is kidnapped
by the Reds who substitute a double for him. Almost all of those who find out are also eliminated.

120   _____. Where No Flags Fly. Chicago: Regnery,
1961.
A refugee scientist agrees to go behind the
Iron Curtain to find out for American Intelligence
when the Soviets will launch their missile attack
on the U.S.

121   Bachmann, Lawrence P. The Bitter Lake. Boston:
Little, Brown, 1970.
A "guest" aboard a freighter stranded in the
Suez Canal during the Six Day War of 1967 is busy
gathering data for British Intelligence.

122   Bagley, Desmond. The Freedom Trap. Garden
City, N.Y.: Doubleday, 1972.

Counter-intelligence agent is sentenced to prison
and then sprung with a Soviet spy. The plan to tail
the man to the source of some secret goodies was
airtight--until someone betrayed it.

123 _____. The Golden Keel. Garden City, N.Y.:
Doubleday, 1964.
Mussolini's missing treasure and a plan to
smuggle it out of Italy.

124 _____. Running Blind. Garden City, N.Y.:
Doubleday, 1971.
Someone tries to kill agent Alan Stewart before
he can deliver a secret electronics unit to an unknown pickup in Iceland.

125 _____. The Tightrope Men. Garden City, N.Y.:
Doubleday, 1973.
Giles Denison agrees to serve as a decoy
scientist while British agents find some secret
papers which will reveal how laser beams can be
projected by X-rays.

126 _____. Wyatt's Hurricane. Garden City, N.Y.:
Doubleday, 1966.
As hurricane flashes down on a Caribbean va-
cationland, only one man can save the inhabitants
from the winds and a schedule revolution.

127 Bahr, Jerome. Holes in the Wall. New York:
McKay, 1970.
A State Department official is captured by the
East Germans for spying. An attempt to gain his
release, leads to a tank confrontation at the Berlin
Wall.

128 Bailey, Anthony. Making Progress. New York: Dial
Press, 1959.
Vacationing at a Swiss resort, English Slater
meets an agent from an Arab country and is offered
a secret mission to Poland. British Intelligence
asks him not to make the trip.

129 Baker, Elliott. Pocock & Pitt. New York: Putnam,
1971. H
A spy farce in which the bored hero, Wendell
Pocock, ditches his family and emerges as the

superspy Winston Pitt.   Sort of a Jekyll and Hyde
of espionage.

130   Baker, Ivon. Grave Doubt. New York: McKay,
       1973. *
              The Heinkel aircraft was another salvage job;
       when the grave of a Luftwaffe airman is opened,
       yesterday's question becomes today's murder--with
       international complications.

131   Baker, Peter. A Killing Affair. Boston: Houghton-
       Mifflin, 1971.
              British attaché in Geneva must read secret
       armaments documents: she falls in love with a
       double agent, who gains some of this data from
       her; she is determined to get it back.

132   Balchin, Nigel M. Sort of Traitor. New York:
       Holt, 1956.
              British scientists discover a way to cure cer-
       tain diseases, but when Whitehall learns the pro-
       cess in reverse can spread germs, it refuses per-
       mission to publish its report. An unscrupulous
       "Publisher" offers to print the account anyway.

133   Ball, John. Mark One: The Dummy. Boston:
       Little, Brown, 1974.
              Edwin Nesbitt, creator of the fictional spy
       Mark Day, employs some of his own hero's
       methods when he is drawn into a real-life espionage
       situation.

134   Ballard, K. G. Gauge of Deception. Garden City,
       N. Y.: Doubleday, 1963.
              American agents investigate the surreptitious
       export of a special gauge from West Berlin.

135   Ballinger, William S. Beacon in the Night. New
       York: Harper, 1959.
              A large number of criminal agents seek to ob-
       tain a map of Balkan oil fields.

136   _____. The Carrion Eaters. New York: Putnam,
       1971.
              International band is caught with its victims in
       a bloody war between Moslems and Hindus on
       Indias's Northwest Frontier.

137   _____. The Spy at Angkor Wat. New York: Put-
       nam, 1965.
            Hawks must uncover a mysterious plot emanating
       from those ancient Cambodian ruins.

138   _____. The Spy in the Java Sea. New York: Put-
       nam, 1965.
            All of his extraordinary linguistic skill, his
       strength, and his mastery of disguise come into
       play as Joaquin Hawks strives to locate a computer
       expert in Djarkarta and get him to repair a crippled
       submarine in the Java Sea before the Communists
       discover its whereabouts.

139   _____. The Spy in the Jungle. New York: Put-
       nam, 1965.
            Another Hawks adventure set in the forests of
       Southeast Asia.

140   Barber, Rowland. The Midnighters. New York:
       Crown, 1970.
            Based on the memoirs of Jewish hero Martin
       Allen Ribakof, this is a "nonfiction novel" showing
       how an "air force" was smuggled into Israel in
       1948.

141   Bartholomew, Cecilia. The Risk. Garden City,
       N. Y.: Doubleday, 1958.
            A family is torn asunder as the father is de-
       clared a security risk during the McCarthy era.

142   Bartram, George. A Job Abroad. New York:
       Macmillan, 1975.
            A middle-aged college professor is given a
       one-time spy job.

143   Bar-Zohar, Michael. The Spy Who Died Twice.
       Transl. by June P. Wilson and Walter B. Michaels.
       Boston: Houghton-Mifflin, 1975.
            Enterprising C. I. A. agent uncovers a Soviet
       spy network leading to the upper echelons of the
       British government.

144   _____. The Third Truth. Transl. by Wilson and
       Michaels. Boston: Houghton-Mifflin, 1973.
            A once top CIA agent is given another chance
       to retrieve his damaged reputation: a multiple

murder case involving the Soviet premier.

145   Barker, Albert. The Apollo Legacy. New York:
        Award, 1971. P
        Reefe King, another paperback James Bond
        type, is drawn into a conspiracy to damage
        America's moon landing missions.

146   _____. Gift From Berlin. New York: Award,
        1969. P
        Reefe King, "righting wrongs."

147   Baron, Stanley W. All My Enemies. New York:
        Ballantine Books, 1953.
        Soviet agent is sent to New York on a secret
        mission, but botches everything up by falling in
        love with the manicurist at his hotel.

148   Barron, Donald. The Man Who Was There. New
        York: Atheneum, 1969.
        The Canfield Institute establishes ideological
        links in nonaligned nations as a cover for its es-
        pionage operations. A chance meeting with an old
        friend in Beirut starts its top operative on a spy
        chase.

149   Barton, Donald R. Once in Aleppo. New York:
        Scribner's, 1955.
        A young American vice-consel in Turaq be-
        comes involved with two girl spies--one U.S. and
        one Russian.

150   Beare, George. The Bee Sting Deal. New York:
        Harper, 1972.
        Residents of the island of Jarma are unhappy
        because their government has entered into a deal
        with Iran for the construction of a road between the
        island and the mainland. An investigative-adven-
        turer and his girlfriend seek to get to the bottom
        of the agreement. Two more are:

151   _____. Bloody Sun at Noon. New York: Harper,
        1970.

152   _____. The Very Breath of Hell. New York:
        Harper, 1971.

153   Beeding, Francis. Twelve Disguises. New York:

Harper, 1942.   *
   The British Intelligence Chief dons a dozen
different disguises to seek a general who has disappeared into German-occupied France.

154   Behn, Noel.   The Kremlin Letter.   New York: Simon
      & Schuster, 1966.
         A Navy Lt. Cmdr is taught all the new espion-
      age techniques and then sent off to Moscow to re-
      cover a message outlining secret agreements for
      detente between the West and a Politburo faction.

155   _____.   The Shadowboxer.   New York: Simon &
      Schuster, 1969.
         A man in 1944 Europe is so completely the lone
      wolf in disguise that he can successfully smuggle
      concentration camp prisoners off the Continent.

156   Bekessy, Jean.   Devil's Agent.   By Hans Habe, pseud.
      Translated by Edward Osers.   New York: Fell,
      1958.   H
         A satirical tale involving an operative who
      spies on both the Russians and the Americans and
      who comes to believe it might be a good deal
      healthier if he can somehow "drop out" of the
      game.

      Bellah, James, coauthor see Stimson, Robert G.

157   Benchley, Nathaniel.   Catch a Falling Spy.   New
      York: McGraw-Hill, 1963.   H
         A funny caper concerning an apparently ordi-
      nary young American couple who earn their living
      spying for the Communist government of Albania.

158   Bennett, Jack.   Ocean Road.   Boston: Little, Brown,
      1967.
         A charter fisherman undertakes a British as-
      signment to organize a counter-revolution against
      a group of Red Chinese-trained Africans who have
      assassinated a sultan and taken over his island
      kingdom.

159   Bennett, Kem.   Devil's Current.   Garden City, N.Y.:
      Doubleday, 1953.
         Someone does not want a young engineer to
      reach Egypt where he is to install a hydroelectric
      plant.

160   _____. Passport for a Renegade. Garden City,
          N. Y. : Doubleday, 1955.
          Agents of Russia and Britain cross swords
          over a defector.

161   Benton, Kenneth. Sole Agent. New York: Walker,
          1974.
          Agent Peter Craig must locate a British girl
          involved with a left-wing group planning the over-
          throw of the Portugese government.

162   _____. Spy in Chancery. New York: Walker,
          1973.
          A Russian spy in Britain's Rome embassy is
          detected;   agent Craig is sent to find out who it is.

163   Bernard, Robert. Illegal Entry. New York: Norton,
          1972.
          An American chemist in England disappears
          and it looks like he has defected.   To solve the
          mystery, his brother must enter Britain illegally.

164   _____. The Ullman Code. New York: Putnam,
          1974.
          A Jewish scholar is employed to decode a
          secret manuscript which may contain the names
          of those who betrayed freedom-fighting partisans
          in the German concentration camps.

165   Bernstein, Kenneth. Intercept. New York: Coward-
          McCann, 1971.
          U. S. reconnaissance plane is downed near the
          Crimean coast;   the two surviving crewmen are
          picked up by the KGB and begin plotting their
          escape.

166   Beste, R. Vernon. The Moonbeams. New York:
          Harper, 1962.
          Agent Maltby is parachuted back into German-
          occupied France charged with finding the traitor in
          his little band of saboteurs.   First published in
          Britain as Faith Has No Country.

167   _____. Next Time I'll Pay My Own Fare. New
          York: Simon & Schuster, 1970.
          A combination spy-detective tale concerning a
          Scotland Yard sleuth's mission to get a former

Nazi out of Spain.

168   _____. Repeat the Instructions. New York: Har-
         per, 1968.
         A British civil servant is used as a pawn by
         Intelligence; he is to "defect" to the Russians,
         while actually serving as a double agent.

169   Bingham, John. The Double Agent. New York:
         Dutton, 1968.
         An Englishman is blackmailed while visiting
         Moscow into supplying data to the Reds. Upon
         his return home, he tells all to British Intelligence,
         which immediately recruits him for a return mis-
         sion to the Soviet Union.

         Black, Gavin, pseud. see Wynd, Oswald

170   Black, Lionel. Arafat Is Next! New York: Stein &
         Day, 1975.
         When an innocent bystander is killed by a
         Palestinian terrorist bomb, his brothers vow to
         kill Arafat in vengeance.

171   _____. The Life and Death of Peter Wade. New
         York: Stein & Day, 1974.
         Johnny Trott is assigned to write a biography
         of a recently-deceased actor whose life was in fact
         a bore. Not so disappointing is the life of Trott's
         ex-wife, the actor's agent, who reveals a link with
         a new African nation where East/West power plays
         are in motion.

172   Blacker, Irwin R. The Kilroy Gambit. Cleveland:
         World, 1960.
         The Russians uncover a "Genops" group in
         Afghanistan and unless the agency's agents can
         reach that remote Asian country in time to cover
         the situation, it will be exposed and destroyed.

         Blair, Charles F., coauthor see Wallis, Arthur J.

173   Blankfort, Michael. The Widow-Makers. New York:
         Simon & Schuster, 1946. *
         When Elliot Green is killed in Lisbon, his
         three children become unwitting possessors of his
         fatal secret.

174 Bloodworth, Dennis. <u>Any Number Can Play</u>. New
York: Farrar, Straus, 1973.
British reporter and his Chinese wife ("Thinking
Lotus") are mixed up with an English agent in the
politically volatile kingdom of Mekong.

175 Boland, John. <u>The Gentlemen at Large</u>. New York:
Award, 1968. P
"The Gentlemen" are an unlikely task force of
ex-Commando officers in the pay of British Intelligence, who must smash a ruthless Communist spy
ring.

176 _____. <u>The Gentlemen Reform</u>. New York:
Award, 1968. P
"Operation Jailbreak" has "the Gentlemen"
freeing a prisoner from a maximum security
British prison.

177 Bonner, Paul. <u>S. P. Q. R.</u> New York: Scribner's,
1952.
The First Secretary of the American embassy
in Rome finds himself hunting a Communist spy.

178 Borden, Mary. <u>Catspaw</u>. New York: Longmans,
Green, 1950. *
Published in Britain as <u>For the Record</u>, this
first-person narrative reveals the growing revulsion
of a young secretary to a European prince, whose
Soviet masters demand he betray his adopted
country.

179 Bottome, Phyllis. <u>Life Line</u>. Boston: Little,
Brown, 1946. *
An English schoolmaster in the Austrian under-
ground fights the Nazis.

180 Boulle, Pierre. <u>Ears of the Jungle</u>. Transl. from
French by Xan Fielding. New York: Vanguard
Press, 1972.
The "jungle" is Southeast Asia, but the "ears"
are the American espionage system that North
Vietnam's intelligence people turn to their own ad-
vantage.

181 _____. <u>A Noble Profession</u>. Transl. from the
French by Xan Fielding. New York: Vanguard

Press, 1961.
The author of Planet of the Apes and Bridge on
the River Kwai here entertains us with the story of
Cousin, an intellectual writer, who enters the secret
service during World War II and grimly achieves
his end of becoming a hero.

182 _____. Not the Glory. Transl. from French by
Xan Fielding. New York: Vanguard Press, 1955.
A decorated veteran of Dunkirk, a novelist,
and a journalist is suspected by British Intelligence
of being the top Nazi agent in the United Kingdom.

183 Bowen, Elizabeth. Heat of the Day. New York:
Knopf, 1948.
In wartime London, a woman's lover turns out
to be a Nazi sympathizer. A British agent in turn
attempts to bring the two--innocent and guilty
alike--to book.

184 Boyle, Kay. A Frenchman Must Die. New York:
Simon & Schuster, 1946.
After the 1944 Liberation, a former Resistance
fighter seeks out a collaborator responsible for the
deaths of many innocents in the village of Savoyard.

185 Brain, Leonard. It's a Free Country. New York:
Coward-McCann, 1966.
Charlie Howard is released from his job in an
electronics firm because he is believed a security
risk. He investigates his investigators and learns
that the same case can truthfully be made against
them.

186 Brelis, Dean. The Mission. New York: Random
House, 1958.
An OSS agent behind Japanese lines in 1943
Burma. The author is a correspondent most
readers have seen with a major American tv net-
work.

187 Brennan, Frederick H. Memo to a Firing Squad.
New York: Knopf, 1943. *
An American newsman and a Polish girl in
Lisbon foil a Nazi plot for a phony peace.

188 Brennan, John. Beware of Midnight. By John

Welcome, pseud.   New York: Knopf, 1962.
A tale of international intrigue involving necro-
mancy and neo-Nazis in Ireland, the Cotswalds,
and Southern Spain.

189 _____. Run for Cover. By John Welcome, pseud.
New York: Knopf, 1960.
A Soviet spy ring attempts to make off with a
stolen manuscript via the French Riviera.

Bridge, Ann, pseud.   see   O'Malley, Mary D.

190 Briley, John.   The Traitors.   New York: Putnam,
1969.
An American patrol in Vietnam is ambushed
and captured by the Viet Cong.   While the survivors are being herded back towards the prison
cages, they are lectured on the "true" history of
the conflict by a Yankee defector.   All of this is
an elaborate setup. . . .

191 Brodeur, Paul.   The Sick Fox.   Boston: Little,
Brown, 1963.
An American agent fails to kill a fox which
bites him one day while he is guarding a secret
underground nuclear storage site in the remote
German countryside.   His failure leads to all sorts
of complications.

192 Brome, Vincent.   The Ambassador and the Spy.   New
York: Crown, 1967.
A desperate man who can prove his British
citizenship is given sanctuary in Britain's legation
in a Soviet satellite nation.   Several times the ambassador's "guest," attempts to escape, but fails.

193 Brook-Shepherd, Gordon.   The Eferding Diaries.
Philadelphia: Lippincott, 1967.
Published in England as The Lion and the Uni-
corn.   Stephen Lane discovers secret documents
which the Soviets want in exchange for incriminating
evidence against him.

194 Brothers, Jay.   Ox.   Indianapolis: Bobbs-Merrill,
1975.   P
Oxford Pomeroy of British Intelligence is being
used--but for what?

195   Brown, Dee A. <u>They Went Thataway</u>. New York:
      Putnam, 1960. H
            In this spoof of TV westerns and spy shows,
      the author of <u>Bury My Heart at Wounded Knee</u>
      shows how a college instructor's PhD dissertation
      is confused with espionage and enemy intelligence
      by an over-zealous secret agent.

      Brown, Harrison, coauthor <u>see</u> Zerwick, Chloe

196   Browne, Gerald. <u>Hazard</u>. New York: Arbor House,
      1973.
            The foiling of an Arab scheme to use a bacter-
      iological superweapon against Israel.

197   Buchan, William. <u>Helen All Alone</u>. New York:
      Morrow, 1962.
            Helen Clark is sent to Senj, the capital of a
      tiny Central European country to keep an eye on
      the children of the British ambassador--and check
      out his activities for Intelligence.

198   Buchanan, James D. <u>The Professional</u>. New York:
      Coward-McCann, 1972.
            Guerin, a professional spy for a semi-official
      U.S. intelligence agency known as "The Firm," is
      sent to Cuba to retrieve some documents and a
      female agent.

199   Buchard, Robert. <u>Thirty Seconds Over New York</u>.
      Transl. from French by June Wilson and Walter
      Michaels. New York: Morrow, 1970. *
            A deranged Chinese colonel places an atomic
      bomb on a converted 707, shoots down the regular
      Paris-to-New-York flight, and substitutes his
      "bomber" for an "under the doormat" attack on Fun
      City.

200   Buckmaster, Henrietta. <u>The Lion in the Stone</u>. New
      York: Harcourt, 1968.
            The Ceylonese U.N. Secretary General, who
      has recently settled the Vietnam conflict, must act
      to prevent a nuclear confrontation between Russian
      and China over Mongolia.

201   Burgess, Anthony. <u>Tremor of Intent</u>. New York:
      Norton, 1966.

A British agent in Yugoslavia receives his final
pre-retirement assignment: bring back from Russia
his old boyhood friend Professor Roper, who has
defected.

202   Burke, Jonathan. Echo of Treason. New York:
       Dodd, Mead, 1966.
       When a wartime traitor is released from prison,
       he decides he ought to write his memoirs; some
       very powerful men, who would rather that he not,
       decide his journalism ought to be halted--perman-
       ently.

203   Burmeister, Jon. Running Scared. New York: St.
       Martin's Press, 1973.
       African President "Tiger" Lunda, a dying man,
       is kidnapped; the kidnapper, also in a mortal con-
       dition, plans to leave the ransom to his wife.

204   Burnett, Hallie. Watch on the Wall. New York:
       Morrow, 1965.
       Visiting Berlin an American girl becomes in-
       volved in a scheme to help an East German escape
       over "The Wall."

205   Burt, Katherine. Captain Millett's Island. New York:
       Macrae, Smith, 1944.   *
       Nazi intrigue on a Caribbean island.

206   Caidin, Martin. Almost Midnight. New York: Mor-
       row, 1971.
       Five nuclear bombs of multi-kiloton force are
       missing and five major American cities will mush-
       room up in smoke unless $100 million is paid to
       the gang who stole them.   An enterprising air
       force/intelligence team sets out to stop them.

207   _____. The Cape. Garden City, N.Y.: Double-
       day, 1971.
       Someone is out to sabotage the launching of an
       American space platform scheduled to beat the Rus-
       sians into orbit.

208   _____. Cyborg. New York: Arbor House, 1972.
       An air force test pilot crashes and is put back

together with artificial parts at a top secret installa-
tion; thus Colonel Steve Austin, the "Six Million
Dollar Man," is sent on an underwater search for
nuclear subs off South America and an anti-Arab
mission with a girl Israeli agent.

209   . Cyborg IV. New York: Arbor House,
       1975.
       Bionic marvel Steve Austin finds himself dis-
patched in a space vehicle to find the source that's
rendering American recon-satellites inoperative.

210   . The God Machine. New York: McKay,
       1968.
       An agent must halt the government's secret
computer that has gone berserk and threatens to
take over the world.

211   . High Crystal. New York: Arbor House,
       1974.
       Austin becomes involved in a race to find the
hidden source of a mysterious laser high in the
Andes and uncover the secret behind the "Chariots
of the Gods."

212   . Operation Nuke. New York: McKay, 1973.
       The "Six Million Dollar Man" must uncover some
tactical nuclear weapons which a group of nasties
are using to blackmail the American government.
A variation on the theme of the author's Almost
Midnight (see 206).

213 Caillou, Alan. Death Charge. New York: Pinnacle
       Books, 1973. P
       Colonel Tobin's private army is the deadliest
force in the world; these mercenaries will fight
wars anywhere. In this adventure, Tobin's people
are sent to Mexico where political kidnappings of
American businessmen have been on the rise; the
terrorists involved are believed to be hiding in the
Sierra Madres. Other tales in this exclusively
paperback series are:

214   . Afghan Assault. New York: Pinnacle
       Books, 1973. P

215   . Congo War Cry. New York: Pinnacle
       Books, 1972. P

216 _____. Dead Sea Submarine. New York: Pinnacle
          Books, 1972. P

217 _____. Swamp War. New York: Pinnacle Books,
          1973. P

218 _____. Terror in Rio. New York: Pinnacle
          Books, 1973. P

219 Callison, Brian. A Plague of Sailors. New York:
          Putnam, 1971.
              An agent must learn who has stolen a new
          brand of killer germs for use against Israel. All
          of the action takes place at sea.

220 Canning, Victor. Doubled in Diamonds. New York:
          Morrow, 1967.
              Our hero must prevent the exchange of stolen
          industrial diamonds for Chinese opium.

221 _____. The Dragon Tree. New York: Sloane,
          1958.
              English major subdues intrigue and nationalism
          on the South American island of Cyrenia.

222 _____. Firecrest. New York: Morrow, 1972.
              Our hero is a research scientist who invents
          a new and rather reasonable secret weapon wanted
          by "The Department," who also want the inventor
          disposed of; he hides it to prolong his life.

223 _____. The Finger of Saturn. New York: Morrow,
          1974.
              Englishman receives word that his missing wife
          is alive and well and with help from an agent, many
          people in many lands become involved.

224 _____. Forrest of Eyes. New York: Mill, 1950.
              English engineer engineers the escape of an
          important anti-Communist VIP from post-war
          Yugoslavia.

225 _____. The Golden Salamander. New York: Mill,
          1949.
              English scholar becomes involved in intrigue
          and murder in the deserts of North Africa.

226 _____. The Great Affair. New York: Morrow,
          1971.

Defrocked clergyman and superspy uses the
funds he gathered from knocking off enemy agents
to build a home for crippled children.

227   ____. A Handful of Silver. New York: Sloane,
        1954.
        A British schoolmaster agrees to work for
Intelligence. His mission is to kidnap and hold
the son of an Eastern potentate until an oil con-
cession is safe.

228   ____. The Limbo Line. New York: Sloane,
        1964.
        First published in Ladies' Home Journal under
the title Margin of Peril. A retired British agent
is reinstated to find "Limbo," the French location
of a reverse underground railway in which Soviet
refugees are kidnapped and returned to Russia.

229   ____. The Mask of Memory. New York: Mor-
        row, 1975.
        Agent Tucker finds a trade unionist conspiracy
to take over the British government.

230   ____. Panther's Moon. New York: Mill, 1948.
        A pair of circus panthers escape; in the collar
of one is an important microdot. British agent
Catherine Talbot wants to recover the beasts before
the Soviets.

231   ____. The Python Project. New York: Morrow,
        1968.
        Private detective involved with British Intelli-
gence, a gang of kidnappers, a foreign government,
the London police, and murder.

232   ____. Queen's Pawn. New York: Morrow, 1969.
A bitter aristocrat, a beautiful woman, and a big-
time thief are all used as pawns by a man named
Sarling, who wants to realize a dream.

233   ____. The Rainbow Pattern. New York: Morrow,
        1973.
        Book One: likeable British con artist tries to
help an old woman trace a long lost illegitimate
nephew; Book Two: agents track down a man who
kidnaps VIPs (the two tales are connected).

234   _____. The Whip Hand. New York: Morrow,
       1965.
       Rex Carver follows a beautiful German blond
       and winds up in a nice old theatrical schloss in the
       Bavarian Alps.

235   Carey, Constance. Chekhov Proposal. New York:
       Putnam, 1975.
       Is Presidential candidate Hoffman a Soviet
       "sleeper" agent?

236   Carter, Lin. The Nemesis of Evil. Garden City,
       N. Y.: Doubleday, 1975.
       Prince Zarkon and his Omega organization are
       pitted against arch-nasty Lucifer.

237   Carter, Nick. Agent Counter-Agent. New York:
       Award, 1973. P
       Super agent hero-narrator, Nick Carter called
       "N-3," or "Killmaster," has survived more capers
       than any other secret operative in literature--paper-
       back or hardbound. In this tale, he plays the role
       of a double agent.

238   _____. Amazon. New York: Award, 1969. P
       "Killmaster" defies death in South America.

239   _____. Amsterdam. New York: Award, 1970. P
       A wanton blonde is the only lead to a private
       spy network.

240   _____. The Arab Plague. New York: Award,
       1970. P
       Carter is exposed to a mind-altering drug and
       a new twist on the slave trade.

241   _____. Assassin: Code Name Vulture. New
       York: Award, 1974. P

242   _____. The Assassination Brigade. New York:
       Award, 1973. P

243   _____. Assault on England. New York: Award,
       1974. P

244   _____. Assignment: Israel. New York: Award,
       1974. P

245   _____. Australia. New York: Award, 1970. P

246   _____. The Aztec Avenger. New York: Award,
       1974. P

247   _____. Beirut Incident. New York: Award,
         1974. P

248   _____. Berlin. New York: Award, 1970.
         A beautiful woman is only lead to a fanatical
         neo-Nazi who looks like Hitler and wants to be the
         new Führer.

249   _____. The Black Death. New York: Award,
         1969. P

250   _____. The Bright Blue Death. New York:
         Award, 1967. P
         "Killmaster" stalks a crazed scientist dedicated
         to destroying the world.

251   _____. A Bullet for Fidel. New York: Award,
         1970. P
         Doomsday weapon in Cuban hands.

252   _____. The Butcher of Belgrade. New York:
         Award, 1973. P

253   _____. The Cairo Mafia. New York: Award,
         1972. P

254   _____. Cambodia. New York: Award, 1970. P

255   _____. Carnival for Killing. New York: Award,
         1969. P

256   _____. Casbah Killers. New York: Award,
         1969. P
         A macabre manhunt for a missing AXE agent.

257   _____. Checkmate in Rio. New York: Award,
         1970. P
         Sex and savagery are the facts of life on this
         mission to Argentina.

258   _____. China Doll. New York: Award, 1969. P
         Carter finds himself the first white man in the
         "Forbidden City" of Peking.

259   _____. The Chinese Paymaster. New York:
         Award, 1970. P
         "N-3" hunts a double agent who has set America
         up for a takeover.

260   _____. The Cobra Kill. New York: Award,
         1974. P
         Carter and a beautiful nymphomaniac on a wild
         manhunt in Malaysia.

261 _____. The Code. New York: Award, 1973. P

262 _____. Code Name Werewolf. New York: Award, 1974. P

263 _____. Danger Key. New York: Award, 1973. P
Mr. Judas returns to settle an old score.

264 _____. Death of the Falcon. New York: Award, 1974. P

265 _____. Death Strain. New York: Award, 1970. P

266 _____. The Death's Head Conspiracy. New York: Award, 1973. P

267 _____. The Defector. New York: Award, 1974. P
Carter obeys the whims of a beautiful spy to keep the U.S. from blowing sky high.

268 _____. The Devil's Cockpit. New York: Award, 1969. P
"N-3" infiltrates a pornographic propaganda mill pledged to pervert the West.

269 _____. The Devil's Dozen. New York: Award, 1973. P

270 _____. Doomsday Formula. New York: Award, 1972. P
Japanese Communists threaten to sink Hawaii.

271 _____. Double Identity. New York: Award, 1972. P
"Killmaster" must eliminate the deadly double who matches him in every skill.

272 _____. Dragon Flame. New York: Award, 1969. P
Hong Kong--a nerve-scorching inferno for an agent who smuggles generals.

273 _____. The Executioners. New York: Award, 1973. P

274 _____. Eyes of the Tiger. New York: Award, 1973. P
Switzerland, a beautiful blond and a golden tiger.

275 _____. The Filthy Five. New York: Award, 1967. P
"Killmaster" races to prevent the assassination of the President.

276   _____. Fourteen Seconds to Hell. New York:
           Award, 1968. P

277   _____. Fraulein Spy. New York: Award, 1970. P
           "N-3" is on the trail of Hitler's right-hand
           man, Martin Bormann.

278   _____. The Golden Serpent. New York: Award,
           1972. P
           Armed with only a suicide pill, "Killmaster"
           must stop the ruin of America's economy.

279   _____. Hanoi. New York: Award, 1968. P
           Impersonating a German scientist, Carter
           crawls deep into North Vietnam.

280   _____. Hood of Death. New York: Award,
           1974. P
           The bait--six beautiful women; the plot--to
           destroy every powerful official in America.

281   _____. Hour of the Wolf. New York: Award,
           1973. P

282   _____. Human Time-Bomb. New York: Award,
           1970. P
           "Killmaster" is faced by a master army of men
           and women, neither dead nor alive!

283   _____. Ice Bomb Zero. New York: Award,
           1971. P

284   _____. Ice Trap Terror. New York: Award,
           1974. P
           "N-3" must destroy an evil colonel and his
           electronic weapons.

285   _____. Inca Death Squad. New York: Award,
           1972. P

286   _____. Istanbul. New York: Award, 1971. P

287   _____. The Jerusalem File. New York: Award,
           1975. P

288   _____. Jewel of Doom. New York: Award,
           1970. P

289   _____. Judas Spy. New York: Award, 1968. P
           Trapped in the treacherous jungles of Indonesia
           by the infamous Mr. Judas.

290   _____. Korean Tiger. New York: Award,
           1967. P

291   _____. Kremlin File. New York: Award,
       1973. P

292   _____. The Liquidator. New York: Award,
       1973. P

293   _____. Living Death. New York: Award,
       1969. P
       A hideous destruction-machine is stealing the
       minds of the world's most brilliant scientists.

294   _____. Macao. New York: Award, 1973. P
       "Killmaster" must lure a depraved beauty into
       a suicide assignment.

295   _____. The Man Who Sold Death. New York:
       Award, 1974. P

296   _____. The Mark of Cosa Nostra. New York:
       Award, 1971. P

297   _____. Massacre in Milan. New York: Award,
       1974. P

298   _____. The Mind Killers. New York: Award,
       1970. P

299   _____. The Mind Poisoners. New York: Award,
       1971. P
       International plot to hook American college
       kids on violence drugs and use them to destroy
       their country.

300   _____. Mission to Venice. New York: Award,
       1971. P

301   _____. Moscow. New York: Award, 1970. P

302   _____. Night of the Avenger. New York: Award,
       1973. P

303   _____. The N3 Conspiracy. New York: Award,
       1974. P

304   _____. The Omega Terror. New York: Award,
       1972. P

305   _____. Operation Che Guevara. New York:
       Award, 1969. P
       The dead guerrilla leader is kept strangely
       alive in a secret kept by two beautiful, treacherous
       women.

306   _____. Operation Moon Rocket. New York:
       Award, 1970. P

America's astronauts are the targets, murdered one by one.

307 _____. Operation Snake. New York: Award, 1969. P
Nightmare mission pits "Killmaster" against a power-mad monk in a global tug-of-war.

308 _____. Operation Starvation. New York: Award, 1966. P

309 _____. Our Agent in Rome Is Missing. New York: Award, 1973. P
Can you guess who is to find him?

310 _____. Paris. New York: Award, 1970. P

311 _____. Peking and the Tulip Affair. New York: Award, 1969. P

312 _____. Peking Dossier. New York: Award, 1974. P

313 _____. Red Guard. New York: Award, 1967. P
Unless "Killmaster" acts fast, the monsters of China's Cultural Revolution will blow up the world.

314 _____. Red Rays. New York: Award, 1969. P
A bizarre new sex ray is being used by the Red Chinese to launch a global death game.

315 _____. Red Rebellion. New York: Award, 1970. P
Chinese operatives on American college campuses.

316 _____. Rhodesia. New York: Award, 1970. P

317 _____. Run Spy Run. New York: Award, 1969. P
From New York to London.

318 _____. Safari for Spies. New York: Award, 1970. P
An explosive assignment in Africa's dark heart.

319 _____. Saigon. New York: Award, 1970. P
Chinese assassination bureau known as "The Bitter Almonds" sends a female agent after Carter.

320 _____. Sea Trap. New York: Award, 1972. P

321 _____. Seven Against Greece. New York: Award, 1973. P

322   _____. Sign of the Cobra. New York: Award,
1974. P

323   _____. The Spanish Connection. New York:
Award, 1973. P

324   _____. Spy Castle. New York: Award, 1971. P
British Intelligence is infiltrated and subverted
for world conquest.

325   _____. Strike Force Terror. New York: Award,
1974. P

326   _____. Target: Doomsday Island. New York:
Award, 1973. P

327   _____. Temple of Fear. New York: Award,
1970. P
"N-3" assumes the identity of a man long dead.

328   _____. The Terrible Ones. New York: Award,
1968. P
"Operation Blast" will move from Dominica to
destroy the U.S., unless....

329   _____. The Thirteenth Spy. New York: Award,
1970. P
Carter is the 13th agent to be sent to Moscow....

330   _____. Time Clock of Death. New York: Award,
1970. P

331   _____. Vatican Vendetta. New York: Award,
1974. P

332   _____. The Weapon of Night. New York: Award,
1971. P
Total annihilation is threatened under the cover
of paralyzing power failures.

333   _____. Web of Spies. New York: Award,
1971. P
Carter is ordered to smash Spain's notorious
espionage group, "The Spiders."

334 Carter, Youngman. Mr. Campion's Farthing. New
York: Morrow, 1969. H*
Russian scientist disappears in England;
Soviet agents are on his tail; British Intelligence
must locate him.

335 Cassill, R. V. Dr. Cobb's Game. New York:

Geis, 1970.
A man with a mission--to save a scandal-rid-
den Britain; as much a look at the occult as a
spy thriller.

Castle, John, pseud. see Payne, Ronald and
John Garrod

336   Catto, Max. The Banana Men. New York: Simon &
Schuster, 1967.
Hurricane Hannah blows a helicopter carrying
the President into the middle of a Cuban swamp.

337   Chacko, David. Gage. New York: St. Martin's
Press, 1974.
Attempts to destroy an espionage outfit in-
volved in domestic political assassinations.

338   Chamales, Thomas. Never So Few. New York:
Scribner's, 1957.
Guerrilla operations in World War II Burma.

339   Charles, Robert. Flight of the Raven. New York:
Pinnacle Books, 1975.

340   _____. The Hour of the Wolf. New York:
Pinnacle Books, 1975.
The first two titles in a new "Counter-Terror"
series in which an international group of good guys
(and girls) must battle a world-wide crowd of
nasties: Terror, Inc.

341   _____. Stamboul Intrigue. New York: Roy, 1968.
During the 1964 Cyprus crisis (the one before
last!), agents are sent to Istanbul to look into re-
ported Soviet schemes to provoke open warfare between Greece and Turkey.

342   Chase, James H. This Is for Real. New York:
Walker, 1967.
Girland is the only agent left to send to Senegal
in search for a colleague now playing for the other
side.

343   _____. You Have Yourself a Deal. New York:
Walker, 1968.
Girland is sent to Paris to find out why a girl

found along the Seine with amnesia had the initials
of a top Chinese agent stenciled across her anatomy.

344   Cheney, Peter. Dark Omnibus. 3 vols. in 1. New
York: Dodd, Mead, 1952. H*
In addition to Sinister Errand (345), this an-
thology includes Dark Street and Stars Are Dark.

345   _____. Sinister Errand. New York: Dodd, Mead,
1945. H*
Amateur courier fumbles his way through a
sophisticated caper to obtain the Russian timetable
for a projected invasion of Yugoslavia.

346   Childers, Erskine. Riddle of the Sands. New York:
Dodd, Mead, 1940. Y*
Two young sailors gain the plans for Germany's
cross-Channel invasion.

347   Childs, Marquis. Taint of Innocence. New York:
Harper, 1967.
Harvard graduate CIA recruit finds himself attempting to keep the oil-rich sheikdom of Sibai out
of Russian hands.

348   Christie, Agatha. N or M? New York: Dodd, Mead,
1941. *
Much better known for her murder mysteries,
this author has managed to slip in a few stories of
intrigue and espionage. In this one, Tommy and
Tuppence Beresford, retired World War I spies,
are called on once more to enter service.

349   _____. Passenger to Frankfurt. New York: Dodd,
Mead, 1971. *
"Project Benvo" is a sinister plot against international peace which must be solved by the Beresfords.

350   _____. Postern of Fate. New York: Dodd, Mead,
1973. *
The Beresfords set off on a dangerous trail
that leads from the mysterious death of a World
War I spy to the present.

351   _____. So Many Steps to Death. New York: Dodd,
Mead, 1955. *

Famous European scientist's disappearance
leads to Morocco.

352 _____. They Came to Baghdad. New York: Dodd,
Mead, 1951. *
Victoria Jones, fired from her London job,
journeys to Baghdad and there becomes a key figure
in a plot against world peace.

353 Christopher, John. Scent of White Poppies. New
York: Simon & Schuster, 1959.
A light suspense thriller set on the Yorkshire
coast replete with complications in the vein of
Helen MacInnes.

354 Clark, William. Number Ten. Boston: Houghton-
Mifflin, 1967.
Power struggle breaks out in the British gov-
ernment, sparked by a crisis in Africa.

355 _____. Special Relationship. Boston: Houghton-
Mifflin, 1969.
In 1977 the new U.S. President agrees to a
CIA plan for unseating the Indian government and
replacing it with a military junta.

356 Clayton, Richard. The Antagonists. By William
Haggard, pseud. New York: Washburn, 1964.
An important Yugoslav scientist in England is
wanted dead-or-alive by certain Russian, British,
and American agents. Colonel Charles Russell of
the Security Executive is charged with his safety.

357 _____. The Arena. By William Haggard, pseud.
New York: Washburn, 1962.
The Security Executive must see if a huge
financial deal in London is a danger to the state.

358 _____. Closed Circuit. By William Haggard,
pseud. New York: Washburn, 1961.
British Foreign Service meddles in the South
American republic of Candoro.

359 _____. The Conspirators. By William Haggard,
pseud. New York: Walker, 1968.
Colonel Russell must find the second of two
atomic bombs accidentally dropped off the coast

of Devon before anti-American elements in Britain
learn of it.

360   _____. A Cool Day for Killing. By William
Haggard, pseud. New York: Walker, 1968.
Agent Russell works to overcome the effects
of a political assassination and a military takeover
in a far-off Malay kingdom.

361   _____. The Hard Sell. By William Haggard,
pseud. New York: Washburn, 1966.
Industrial espionage and murder in the produc-
tion of a British aircraft engine which could mean
millions for Britain in competition with America.

362   _____. The Hardliners. By William Haggard,
pseud. New York: Walker, 1971.
Retired from the Security Executive, Russell
must dissuade a prominent author from writing a
book on a Central European nation.

363   _____. The High Wire. By William Haggard,
pseud. New York: Washburn, 1963.
An indiscreet remark leads to involvement with
spies; Russell saves the day.

364   _____. The Powder Barrel. By William Haggard,
pseud. New York: Washburn, 1965.
Russell must work together with a Soviet agent
to prevent an explosive crisis in a Mideast oil
sheikhdom ripe for anarchy.

365   _____. The Power House. By William Haggard,
pseud. New York: Washburn, 1967.
Russell is faced with interlocking problems
which threaten Britain's Establishment and way-of-
life.

366   _____. Slow Burner. By William Haggard, pseud.
Boston: Little, Brown, 1958.
Physicist heads up a search for a nuclear device sending strange rays from a modest private
building in a London suburb.

367   _____. The Telemann Touch. By William Haggard,
pseud. Boston: Little, Brown, 1959.
The British have discovered oil beneath a

Caribbean island, want to retain it in the Common-
wealth and send their man to insure things run
smoothly; a competitor arrives to liquidate him.

368   _____. Too Many Enemies. By William Haggard,
pseud. New York: Walker, 1972.
An incorruptible Member of Parliament and an
Arab agent and assassin cross swords with Colonel
Russell.

369   _____. Venetian Blind. By William Haggard,
pseud. New York: Washburn, 1960.
Secrets leak from a British industrial plant.

370 Cleary, Jon. The High Commissioner. New York:
Morrow, 1967.
A cross between a spy and detective story: an
Australian sleuth is to arrest the High Commissioner for murder; in London, he finds the man
involved in negotiations to end the Vietnam War and
must protect him.

371   _____. The Long Pursuit. New York: Morrow,
1967.
Englishmen and women join a guerrilla band
in 1942 Sumatra.

372   _____. Season of Doubt. New York: Morrow,
1968.
American embassy official in Lebanon attempts
to dissuade a friend in the gunrunning business.
Other tales include:

373   _____. Fall of an Eagle. New York: Morrow,
1964.

374   _____. Forests of the Night. New York: Morrow,
1970.

375   _____. North From Thursday. New York: Morrow, 1969.

376   _____. Pulse of Danger. New York: Morrow,
1966.

377 Cleeve, Brian. Death of a Bitter Englishman. New
York: Random House, 1967.
"The Agency" has had a recent change in com-
mand and the former Director asks Sean Ryan to

investigate agent's death officially listed as a suicide.

378 _____. Vice Isn't Private. New York: Random
House, 1966.
Ryan's arranges the escape of a convicted murderer planning to blackmail the British Home Secretary and pursue him in an effort to prevent the
plan. Two other Agent Ryan stories are:

379 _____. Escape from Prague. New York: Random
House, 1970.

380 _____. Vote X for Treason. New York: Random
House, 1964.

381 Clements, Eileen H. Cherry Harvest. London:
Messner, 1944. Y*
RAF Intelligence officer breaks a German espionage ring operating out of an English girls'
school.

382 Clewes, Howard. Epitaph for Love. Garden City,
N. Y. : Doubleday, 1953.
An English resident of Italy meets a girl years
after their short love affair and joint work in the
wartime Resistance. Unfortunately, they meet as
enemies in an espionage plot.

383 Clifford, Francis. All Men Are Lonely Now. New
York: Coward-McCann, 1967. *
An East German discloses a secret laser-
guided missile; Britain's Ministry of Defence is
investigated.

384 _____. The Hunting Ground. New York: Coward-
McCann, 1964. *
A photographer is the sole witness to a plane
crash shrouded in official silence.

385 _____. The Naked Runner. New York: Coward-
McCann, 1966. *
Ex-agent on a minor courier assignment is
captured by East Germans; under threat of his
son's death, he is forced to become their assassin.
Two more stories are:

386 _____. Another Way of Dying. New York:

Coward-McCann, 1969.

387 _____. Blind Side. New York: Coward-McCann, 1971.

Coles, Henry, coauthor see Manning, Adelaide F. O.

Coles, Manning, pseud. see Manning, Adelaide F. O. and Henry Coles

388 Collingwood, Charles. The Defector. New York: Harper, 1970. *
　　Veteran CBS correspondent tells of the adventures of a "colleague" persuaded by the CIA to make a trip to North Vietnam and contact a Hanoi official rumored to be interested in defecting.

389 Collins, Norman. The Bat That Flits. Boston: Little, Brown, 1953.
　　Top-secret laboratory in a remote part of Cornwall.

390 Condon, Richard. The Manchurian Candidate. New York: McGraw-Hill, 1959.
　　Raymond was Red China's deadliest weapon-- an all American hero programed to assassinate upon command.

391 _____. The Star Spangled Crunch. New York: Bantam Books, 1974. PH
　　A satirical spy story in which a power-mad but wacky gang of schemers plot the world's slickest takeover.

392 _____. Winter Kills. New York: Dial Press, 1974.
　　The family of President Tim Kegan is forced by a deathbed confession to reopen the investigation into his assassination and the ensuing trail leads almost everywhere including inside the CIA; obviously modeled on the Kennedy tragedy.

393 Connable, Alfred. Twelve Trains to Babylon. Boston: Little, Brown, 1971.
　　CIA agent to answer the question: "Is the Mafia planning to take over a secret Communist espionage organization operating inside this country?"

394 Cooke, David C. % American Embassy. New York:
   Dodd, Mead, 1967.
    Likeable CIA agent is sent to New Delhi to
   find out why a recently deceased beggar had a
   number of perfect counterfeit ten-rupee notes.

395 Cooney, Michael. Doomsday England. New York:
   Walker, 1966.
    The Queen's Investigator is the hereditary head
   of H. M. Secret Service. Using the tools of his
   trade--money, sex and violence--he must find and
   disarm a monster cobalt bomb planted somewhere
   in England by the Russians.

306 Cooper, Brian. A Touch of Thunder. New York:
   Vanguard, 1962.
    An intelligence officer in the old Indian army
   seeks to prevent Gandhi's less-peaceful followers
   from blowing up a section of the Calcutta-Peshawar
   railway.

397 _____. The Van Langeren Girl. New York:
   Vanguard, 1961.
    Set in India towards the close of the war; a
   beautiful Eurasian girl is suspected of being a
   Japanese spy.

398 Copeland, William. Five Hours from Isfahan. New
   York: Putnam, 1975.
    American agent in 1943 Teheran involved in
   the real-life German plot to assassinate Roosevelt,
   Churchill, and Stalin.

399 Coppel, Alfred. Thirty-Four East. New York:
   Harcourt, 1974.
    The dusty desert of the Sinai Peninsula is the
   locale of an unexpected superpower confrontation.

400 Cordell, Alexander. The Deadly Eurasian. New
   York: Weybright & Talley, 1969.
    A Chinese spy story, first published in Britain
   as The Bright Cantonese. A Red Guard agent is
   sent by the Party to discover the facts behind the
   launching of a U. S. destroyer's atomic missile.

401 Cory, Desmond. Even If You Run. Garden City,
   N. Y. : Doubleday, 1972.

More character than action in this story of a
young naive spy sent out to Spain from England to
help three hardened agents.

402 _____. Feramontov. New York: Walker, 1966.
Agent Johnny Fedora is ordered to a vacation
spot on the English coast to investigate one Ortiz.

403 _____. Johnny Goes West. New York: Walker,
1958.
Fedora in South America to secure a rich lode
of uranium-bearing carnotite.

404 _____. Mountainhead. New York: Walker, 1968.
Fedora rescues survivors of a plane crash in
Chinese-occupied Tibet.

405 _____. Sunburst. New York: Walker, 1972.
Agent Fedora is sent to quash nuclear blackmail by the Spanish military against other European
governments.

406 _____. Undertow. New York: Walker, 1963.
Fedora in Spain vs. a Soviet agent.

407 Cotter, Gordon. The Cipher. New York: Random
House, 1961.
A visiting American Egyptologist is offered a
large sum to do a deciphering. In so doing, he
learns of a plot to kill the prime minister of a
Mideast oil kingdom. Basis of the Gregory Peck
movie Arabesque.

408 Coulter, Stephen. Embassy. New York: Coward-
McCann, 1971.
The U.S. embassy in Paris is a lively place,
what with defecting Russians, mad assassins,
traitorous staff members, tourists, reporters,
anti-war demonstrators--and the French. Could
Soviet turncoats be smuggled out through that mob?

409 Coxe, George H. Assignment in Guiana. New York:
Knopf, 1942. *
Mysterious deaths and narrow escapes in war-
time South America.

410 _____. Murder in Havana. New York: Knopf,
1943. *
An American engineer in Cuba finds that almost

everyone wants the papers in his briefcase.

411   Craig, David. Message Ends. New York: Stein &
       Day, 1969.
       "Negotiate Now" propaganda demanding that
       Britain capitulate to the Soviet-Bonn Block threatens
       her economic and military independence.

412   _____. Young Men May Die. New York: Stein &
       Day, 1970.
       A nasty adventurer pops up here and there re-
       cruiting other nasties for an unspecified operation.
       British agents are ordered to track him down and
       learn what is coming off.

413   Craig, John. In Council Rooms Apart. New York:
       Putnam, 1971.
       Frank Ridley is drawn out of retirement to
       discover why the Nazis are allowing the hugh troop
       liners Queen Mary and Queen Elizabeth free passage
       across the war-torn Atlantic.

414   Craig, William. The Strasbourg Legacy. New York:
       Crowell, 1975.
       An American agent fights to prevent the restor-
       ation of the Nazi inner circle to power.

415   _____. The Tashkent Crisis. New York: Dutton,
       1971.
       In this doomsday spy story, the President is
       dialed up on the hot line by the Soviet premier and
       ordered to surrender America in 72 hours--or
       Washington will be destroyed by a Soviet laser
       weapon.

416   Creasey, John. Affair for the Baron. By Anthony
       Morton, pseud. New York: Walker, 1968.
       Agents seek both the Baron and a girl he is
       protecting, a girl holding a secret potentially
       damaging to mankind.

417   _____. The Blight. New York: Walker, 1964.   *
       Although better known, like Christie, for his
       murder mysteries, this author has also written a
       few spy volumes. This story concerns one Dr.
       Palfrey, who must find out why certain nasties
       are causing a mysterious blight destroying the

world's timber supply.

418   _____. Dangerous Journey. New York: McKay,
          1974.
          First published during World War II (and an
          excellent example of wartime espionage stories it
          is), this tale concerns British agents Bruce Mur-
          dock and Mary Dell, who are hot on the trail of
          top Nazi spy Kurt von Romain.

419   _____. Dead or Alive. New York: Popular Li-
          brary, 1974. P
          When the possessor of vital defense secrets
          and his daughter are abducted, a suave British
          spy is assigned to rescue them.

420   _____. Death Round the Corner. New York:
          Popular Library, 1969. P
          The head of Britain's counter-intelligence unit
          is drawn into a struggle with a master criminal
          with plans for world conquest.

421   _____. The Famine. New York: Walker, 1967. *
          Dr. Palfrey and his staff at Z5 (the interna-
          tional organization to promote peace) must find
          some man-eating rabbit-like creatures that some
          evil genius has turned loose on the world.

422   _____. I Am the Withered Man. New York:
          Washburn, 1973. *
          Nazi agent von Horssell is sent to Vichy France
          to kidnap a French journalist. The mission will
          also give him a chance to get revenge on the Bri-
          tish operatives. First published in 1941 (see also
          427, 428).

423   _____. The Plague of Silence. New York:
          Walker, 1961. *
          Someone has purposefully loosed a dangerous
          epidemic on the world; Dr. Palfrey must find out
          who is responsible and effect a cure as well.

424   _____. Secret Errand. New York: McKay,
          1974. *
          Beautiful and very dangerous! That was how
          British Intelligence rated actress Felice Damon
          when it ordered Bruce Murdock to find out what

she was up to.   First published during World War
II.

425   _____. The Sleep. New York: Walker, 1964.   *
An African blackmailer attempts to use a form
of sleeping sickness for world domination.   Dr.
Palfrey is needed. . . .

426   _____. The Terror. New York: Walker, 1966.   *
The Supreme International Body is concerned
over a UFO approaching Earth.   The Americans
are convinced it is a Russian nuclear bomb;   the
Russians think it is an American one.   Palfrey is
convinced that it comes from someplace else
(China?). . . .

427   _____. Where Is the Withered Man? New York:
McKay, 1974.   *
A close friend of Hitler's, Nazi agent Kurt von
Romain walks with great difficulty.   Discovering
he was alive and well in Britain, Murdock and
Dell had to stop him (see also 430).   First pub-
lished during the War.

428   _____. The Withered Man. New York: McKay,
1974.   *
Murdock and Dell must stop von Romain before
he can be of aid in Hitler's planned invasion of
1940.   First published during the War.   More of
Creasey's Dr. Palfrey stories include:

429   _____. The Depths. New York: Walker, 1966.   *

430   _____. The Executioners. New York: Walker,
1967.   *

431   _____. The Flood. New York: Walker, 1956.   *

432   _____. The Inferno. New York: Walker,
1965.   *

433   _____. The Menace. New York: Walker,
1958.   *

434   _____. The Oasis. New York: Walker, 1970.   *

435   _____. Perilous Country. New York: Walker,
1966.   *

436   _____. The Smog. New York: Walker, 1970.   *

437   _____. The Touch of Death. New York: Walker,
             1969. *

438   Crosby, John. An Affair of Strangers. New York:
        Stein & Day, 1975.
             Love between an Arab terrorist and an Israeli
        agent.

439   _____. Contract on the President. New York:
             Dell, 1973. P
             One of those combination Mafia-hunting/secret
        agent yarns now much in vogue in paperback. In
        this one, a contract is out to kill the President.

        Cross, James, pseud. see Parry, Hugh J.

440   Crossen, Kendell F. Once Upon a Crime. By
        Christopher Monig, pseud. New York: Dutton,
        1959.

441   _____. So Dead the Rose. By Christopher Monig,
        pseud. New York: Rinehart, 1959.

442   Cussler, Clive. Iceberg. New York: Dodd, Mead,
        1975.
             The failure of a deep-sea probe leads investi-
        gators to a world-wide conspiracy in Iceland.

443   _____. The Mediterranean Caper. New York:
             Pyramid, 1973. P
             A U.S. Naval Intelligence troubleshooter
        searches for the cause behind the sabotage of a
        research vessel.

444   DaCruz, Daniel. Vulcan's Hammer. New York:
        New American Library, 1967.
             Lincoln Blackwood was the almost anonymous
        brain behind the MITRE anti-ballistic missile sys-
        tem, but was he worth the $5 million his kidnappers
        wanted?

445   Daniels, Norman. Operation "K". New York:
        Pyramid, 1966. P
             John Keith, the "Man from A.P.E."--super

secret American agent--is pitted against Red China
in an extraordinary effort to preserve world peace.
Other "Man from A. P. E. " stories are:

446   _____. The Baron of Hong Kong. New York:
         Pyramid, 1966. P

447   _____. Operation "N. " New York: Pyramid,
         1966.

448   _____. Operation "T. " New York: Pyramid,
         1967.

449   _____. Operation "VC. " New York: Pyramid,
         1967.

450   Dark, James. Assignment Tokyo. New York:
         New American Library, 1965.
              "Intertrust" agent Mark Hood unravels the plot
         of a power-hungry genius to infiltrate the Japanese
         nerve-center of a vital secret operation in the
         Anglo-American defense system.

451   _____. Spying Blind. New York: New American
         Library, 1959.
              Agent Hood must hijack a Russian moon-probe.
         Other Agent Hood works are:

452   _____. Assignment Hong Kong. New York: New
         American Library, 1966.

453   _____. Bamboo Bomb. New York: New American
         Library, 1965.

454   _____. Come Die With Me. New York: New
         American Library, 1965.

455   _____. Operation Scuba. New York: New
         American Library, 1971.

456   _____. Sword of Genghis Khan. New York: New
         American Library, 1967.

457   _____. Throne of Satan. New York: New Ameri-
         can Library, 1967.

458   Davidson, Lionel. Night of Wenceslas. New York:
         Harper, 1961.
              Nicholas Whistler, apparently aimless and wit-
         less, is catapulted out of his mundane London life
         to the intrigue of Prague as the naive carrier of
         secret nuclear data.   Two other Davidson tales are:

459   _____. Menorah Men. New York: Harper, 1966.

460   _____. Rose of Tibet. New York: Harper, 1962.

Davies, Frederic, author see Holly, J. Hunter

461   Davis, Dorothy S. Enemy and Brother. New York:
      Scribner's, 1967.
             Set in Greece; a prosecuter and the man he
      jailed unjustly for murder join forces to find the
      answer to an even larger miscarriage of justice
      threatening the security of their land.

462   _____. The Pale Betrayer. New York: Scribner's,
      1966.
             A brilliant young English teacher at a New
      York university delivers her best friend, an impor-
      tant scientist, into the hands of nasty enemy agents.

463   Davis, Maggie. Rommel's Gold. Philadelphia:
      Lippincott, 1971.
             Four young Americans are sent to explore
      Tunisia for a fabled cache of gold buried by "The
      Desert Fox."

464   Day, Gina. Tell No Tales. New York: Stein & Day,
      1968.
             Lady agent trails a handsome traitor.

465   Dean, Elizabeth. Murder a Mile High. Garden City,
      N.Y.: Doubleday, 1944. *
             Emma Marsh tails enemy agents in wartime
      Colorado.

466   Dean, Robert G. Pinned Man. By George Griswold,
      pseud. Boston: Little, Brown, 1955.
             British and American Intelligence cooperate in
      tracking down a dangerous Communist operative in
      Switzerland.

467   _____. Red Pawns. By George Griswold, pseud.
      New York: Dutton, 1954.
             Superagent Mr. Groode becomes involved in a
      Mideast intrigue.

468   DeGramont, Sanche. Lives to Give. New York:
      Putnam, 1971.

Four Resistance fighters are summoned to a secret meeting--only to be met at the door by the Gestapo.

469   Deighton, Len. The Billion Dollar Brain. New York: Putnam, 1966.
British secret agent is recruited into a computer-based espionage unit presided over by rich but evil Texan General Midwinter. Michael Caine starred in the movie.

470   _____. An Expensive Place to Die. New York: Putnam, 1967.
An anonymous British agent is made personally responsible for heading off a catastrophe born of an American lie and maturing rapidly into the imminent explosion of a Chinese hydrogen bomb.

471   _____. Funeral in Berlin. New York: Putnam, 1965.
In what is probably this author's most famous work, a British agent smuggles a Russian scientist out of East Berlin with the connivance of a Soviet security officer. Michael Caine in the movie again.

472   _____. Horse Under Water. New York: Putnam, 1968.
An agent attempts against various opposition to salvage Nazi-forged currency from a German submarine sunk off the Portugese coast during the War.

473   _____. The Ipcress File. New York: Simon & Schuster, 1964.
Our no-name spy hero maneuvers his way through the murky world of international espionage in the Near East, the Pacific, and behind the Iron Curtain, always knowing exactly what he is doing and for which "side" he is operating. Michael Caine starred in the movie.

474   _____. Spy Story. New York: Harcourt, 1974.
A British agent is assigned to the employ of a joint Anglo-American naval warfare committee. His orders include a bit of spying for his old employer and assisting the defection of a Soviet admiral.

475   Dekker, Anthony. Temptation in a Private Zoo. New
       York: Morrow, 1970.
          In this Cold War Bondish yarn, a British public
       relations man is enmeshed at Bear Garden, osten-
       sibly a management-training school run by the Ger-
       man Gersachs Group for its English staff.

476   Dembo, Samuel. Kalahari Kill. New York: Morrow,
       1964.
          Intelligence operative Brady is ordered to
       Africa to locate the notorious Otto Hulsenbeck, a
       Gestapo leader who escaped the Allies at the close
       of the War.

       Derby, Mark, pseud. see Wilcox, Harry

477   DeVilliers, Gerald.   Angel of Vengeance. New York:
       Pinnacle, 1974. P
          Malko is one of the CIA's most daring and ef-
       fective "special" agents--the man who gets the im-
       possible missions, the dirty jobs, and the secret
       operations that demand the coolness of a million-
       dollar caper and the finality of a commando hit.
       In this first of a new and exclusively paperback
       series, our hero must hijack a helicopter from the
       Uruguayan army, disguise its markings, and force
       the pilot to fly him into a prison courtyard where
       he can rescue an important political hostage.

478   _____. Kill Kissinger. New York: Pinnacle,
       1974. P
          Our hero is ordered to prevent just such a
       plot.

479   _____. The Man From Kabul. New York:
       Pinnacle, 1974. P

480   _____. Operation New York. New York: Pinnacle,
       1974. P
          A plot to bring harm to certain residents of
       Gotham.

481   _____. Que Viva Guevara. New York: Pinnacle,
       1975. P
          A U.S. vice President is to be killed during a
       tour of Latin America, unless....

482   _____. Versus the CIA. New York: Pinnacle,
       1974. P

483   _____. West of Jerusalem. New York: Pinnacle,
         1974. P
             As one reads on in this series, other interest-
         ing things about the background of this hero begin
         popping out. Item: Agent Malko is in fact an
         Austrian nobleman, Prince Malko Linge. Item:
         He works for the CIA in order to earn enough cash
         to restore his ancestral castle. Item: In this
         story, he is involved in a plot to damage the na-
         tional security of Israel.

484   DeVoto, Bernard A. Advance Agent. By John
         August, pseud. Boston: Little, Brown, 1942. *
             A soldier and a journalist expose a secret Nazi
         sabotage organization. For sex, violence, and
         general mayhem does not hold a candle to the likes
         of James Bond.

485   Diment, Adam. The Bang, Bang Birds. New York:
         Dutton, 1969.
             Philip McAlpine of British Intelligence is or-
         dered to help his American colleagues check out the
         Aviary Club of Sweden--sort of an advanced Play-
         boy Club.

486   _____. The Dolly, Dolly Spy. New York: Dutton,
         1968.
             McAlpine, assigned to fly an ex-Nazi out of
         Egypt and hand him over to the Americans, finds
         others interested, retires to Greece to bargain for
         the best price.

487   _____. The Great Spy Race. New York: Dutton,
         1968.
             McAlpine is directed to a tiny island in the
         Indian Ocean where resides a retired spymaster.
         From the old man, he learns of "The Great Spy
         Race," in which he will participate with "contes-
         tants" from all over the world in a contest in
         which the one who outwits all the rest will receive
         the prize: a secret microfilm and a cash fortune.

488   Dipper, Alan. The Golden Virgin. New York:
         Walker, 1973.
             A physicist is working on a secret project for
         Britain when saboteurs try to grab his accumulated
         data.

489   Disney, Dorothy C. 17th Letter. New York: Random
        House, 1945. Y*
        A husband-and-wife detective firm involved in a
        wartime espionage caper in Canada.

490   Divine, Arthur D. Tunnel From Calais. By David
        Rame, pseud. New York: Macmillan, 1943. Y*
        A Royal Navy Intelligence officer and a civilian
        engineer work to block the Germans from tunneling
        under the Channel.

491   Dodge, David. Lights of Sharo. New York: Random
        House, 1954. *
        Once inside a Communist nation, Western news-
        men are not permitted to leave--alive!

492   _____. Troubleshooter. New York: Macmillan,
        1972.
        Two stories involving the same U.S. agent.
        In the first, he is investigated after returning from
        three years' imprisonment in China; in the second,
        he is sent to South Africa where a black insurrec-
        tion is planned against that nation's white rulers.

493   Dodson, Daniel B. The Man Who Ran Away. New
        York: Dutton, 1961.
        American expatriate unknowingly assists in a
        man's abduction from the U.S. to the torture
        chambers of Dictator Torillo in the Caribbean.

494   Dolinger, Foy. The Orange Air. New York: Scrib-
        ner's, 1961.
        Ex-baseball player Hank Easter travels to
        Castro's Cuba and there becomes involved in in-
        trigue against the regime.

495   _____. Sandra Rifkin's Jewels. New York: New
        American Library, 1966. H
        In this overly sex-laden parody of a secret
        agent yarn, Joel Bayside is commissioned by
        Castro to recover some ex-Cuban jewels.

496   Downes, Donald C. The Easter Dinner. New York:
        Rinehart, 1960.
        Italian anti-Fascists plus a pair of American
        secret agents sit down to 1944 Easter dinner.
        Unbeknownst to the spies, the main course consists

of the carrier pigeons they employ to send messages
and intelligence to higher headquarters.

497   _____. Red Rose for Maria. New York: Rine-
        hart, 1960.
        Jules Dellman, an Allied agent, makes use of
        a homely Italian schoolmistress to gather intelli-
        gence for the Salerno and Monte Cassino operations.

498   Downes, Hundon. The Spium Strategem. New York:
        Bantam Books, 1973. P
        Through 256 pages of ceaseless violence, you
        will see the CIA, the Mafia, the Kuomingtang, local
        bandit rulers, Communist and American officials
        all fighting in a warless Southeast Asia for control
        of the real-life Golden Triangle, the greatest white
        poppy area in the world.

499   Driscoll, Peter. In Connection with Kilshaw. Phila-
        delphia: Lippincott, 1974.
        Posing as a reporter, a British agent is off to
        Ulster to eliminate a militant Protestant extremist
        leader.

500   Drury, Allen. The Promise of Joy. Garden City,
        N. Y.: Doubleday, 1975.
        Switches on "Come Nineveh, Come Tyre" by
        having Edward Jason and Mrs. Knox assassinated
        and Orrin Knox ascending to the Presidency at a
        time when the U.S. is mediating an atomic war
        between Russia and China. Lots of intrigue.

501   _____. A Shade of Difference. Garden City,
        N. Y.: Doubleday, 1962.
        Sort of a U.N. "Advise and Consent," in which
        the Harvard-educated ruler of a small African
        country makes trouble for America when he is in-
        volved in a racial incident in Charleston, S. C.

502   _____. The Throne of Saturn. Garden City,
        N. Y.: Doubleday, 1970.
        America's race to Mars and passionate con-
        flicts between astronauts are only part of the story
        as Soviet agents are lurking about attempting to
        put monkey wrenches into the Yankee endeavor.

503   Dryer, Bernard V. Image Makers. New York:

Harper, 1958.
     Dr. Adams, a renowned plastic surgeon, feels
sorrow for certain deaths he believes he caused in
his family.   Flying to Paris for peace and reflec-
tion, he is swept into a dangerous adventure with
the rebel leaders of French Algeria and Morocco.

504   Dulles, Allen, ed.   Great Spy Stories from Fiction.
        New York: Harper, 1969.   *Y
             A collection of 32 examples of spy stories
        drawn from famous espionage novels.   To be com-
        pared with Eric Ambler's work, no. 67.

505   Duncan, Robert L.   The Day the Sun Fell.   By James
        H. Roberts, pseud.   New York: Morrow, 1970.
             Three American soldiers are dropped near
        Nagasaki, shortly before the second A-bomb is
        scheduled to be dropped, with orders to persuade
        the local Catholic bishop to evacuate the city.

506   _____. Dragons at the Gate.   New York: Morrow,
        1975.
             International intrigue and a double double-cross.

507   _____. The February Plan.   By James H. Roberts,
        pseud.   New York: Morrow, 1967.
             Arriving in Tokyo to investigate the U.S. Army's
        official version of his son's death, a well-known
        American writer stumbles onto a monstrous plot by
        Yankee superpatriots to launch an unauthorized at-
        tack on Communist China.

508   _____. The Q Document.   By James H. Roberts,
        pseud.   New York: Morrow, 1964.
             A blend of James Bond and the Bible in which
        agents of various nations attempt to obtain a docu-
        ment potentially damaging to the faith of millions.

509   Dunnett, Dorothy.   Murder in Focus.   Boston:
        Houghton-Mifflin, 1973.
             Three scientists photographing the stars find
        themselves with film that somehow includes secret
        messages wanted by certain nasties.

510   Durrell, Lawrence.   White Eagles Over Serbia.   New
        York: Criterion Books, 1957.
             A veteran British agent discovers the secret

of an outlaw Royalist band attempting to overthrow
Yugoslavia's Tito.

511   Dwyer, K. R.   Dragonfly.   New York: Random House,
       1975.
           A Chinese youth whose body is filled with bu-
       bonic bacilli is programmed to infect his nation and
       must be stopped before a nuclear response is un-
       leashed.

512   Early, Charles.   The Tigers Are Hungry.   New York:
       Morrow, 1968.
           An American air force officer having spent 13
       years in a Russian prison is released by a group
       planning a coup d'état, on condition that he help
       them.

513   Eastwood, James.   The Chinese Visitor.   New York:
       Coward-McCann, 1966.
           A resourceful and beautiful American-Hungarian
       girl is so deeply mixed up in an espionage caper that
       when the boys from Intelligence finally catch up with
       her, they have no choice but to take her into partner-
       ship and follow her leads.   Two other Eastwoods are:

514   _____.   Diamonds Are Deadly.   New York:
       Coward-McCann, 1970.

515   _____.   Little Dragon From Peking.   New York:
       Coward-McCann, 1967.

516   Eberhart, Mignon.   Man Next Door.   New York:
       Random House, 1943.   *
           Nazi spies and saboteurs infest Washington.

517   _____.   Wings of Fear.   New York: Random
       House, 1945.   *
           An American girl and her boyfriend seek Nazi
       spies in Mexico.

518   Ebert, Virginia.   Broken Image.   New York: Morrow,
       1951.
           While awaiting her trial for treason, an Ameri-
       can woman reveals how she became involved with a
       plot to sell a secret code.

519   Edelman, Maurice. A Call on Kuprin. Philadelphia:
       Lippincott, 1960.
           An English-educated Russian scientist helps to
       put a Soviet in space. A "move" is then undertaken
       by British Intelligence to persuade him to return to
       Britain.

520   _____. Dream of Treason. Philadelphia: Lippin-
       cott, 1955.
           The superiors of a Foreign Office agent order
       him to plant some misleading data in the French
       Communist press. They then promptly die in an
       airplane crash, leaving him to face alone the prob-
       lems resulting from their instructions.

521   Eden, Matthew. Conquest Before Autumn. New York:
       Abelard-Schuman, 1973.
           A journalist is due for lunch with his old friend,
       the recently resigned American Defense Secretary,
       but the diplomat has been kidnapped and U.S. stra-
       tegy for an upcoming conference with the Russians
       is endangered.

522   _____. Flight of Hawks. New York: Abelard-
       Schuman, 1971.
           When an American jet with nuclear bombs
       crashes into Russia, a retired CIA man is called
       back to work with the KGB.

523   Egleton, Clive. The Bormann Brief. New York:
       Coward-McCann, 1974.
           A daring attempt is made by a band of Ameri-
       can and British commandos to assassinate Hitler's
       imfamous deputy and thereby throw the already fal-
       tering Nazi High Command into total disarray.
       Reads like McLean.

524   _____. Skirmish. New York: Coward-McCann,
       1975.
           Intrigue, treachery, and international petro-
       politics: the assassination of an Arab Sheikh must
       be stopped.

525   Elegant, Robert S. A Kind of Treason. New York:
       Holt, 1966.
           A best selling author and syndicated columnist

has run out of ideas. A group called QUEST hires
him to learn "the truth about Vietnam," but he must
do a little spying for the CIA on the side.

526   Elwood, Roger and Sam Moskowitz, ed. Great Spy
       Novels and Stories. New York: Pyramid,
       1966. P Y*
              Contains excerpts from various authors cited
       in this Bibliography.

527   Erdman, Paul E. The Billion Dollar Sure Thing.
       New York: Scribner's, 1973.
              An international finance thriller featuring a mul-
       titude of agents--yes, Virginia, even the Mafia has
       spies--a U.S.-Soviet gold struggle, and an Ameri-
       can plan for a new idea in money.

       Esdaile, David, pseud. see Walker, David

       Estabrooks, George H., coauthor see Lockridge,
       Richard

528   Evans, Kenneth. Oasis of Fear. New York: Roy,
       1968.
              Thirty years after the Western Desert Cam-
       paign, a British construction engineer supplements
       his income by aiding the Arabs in various dangerous
       smuggling operations.

529   Falkirk, Richard. The Chill Factor. Garden City,
       N.Y.: Doubleday, 1971.
              British agent is ordered to help the Americans
       uncover a spy ring in Iceland.

530   Fallon, Martin. The Keys of Hell. New York:
       Abelard-Schuman, 1965.
              Paul Chavasse is sent to the forbidden swamps
       of the Albanian coast to find the Black Madonna of
       Scutari, a symbol of hope to the locals which the
       Communists have sworn to destroy.

531   Farr, Finis. The Elephant Valley. New Rochelle,
       N.Y.: Arlington House, 1968.
              A top CIA agent is assigned to discover who
       has blown up an atomic plant in New York and

may want to start World War III.

532   Fast, Charles. Presidential Agent: Ride the Golden
       Tiger. New York: Lancer Books, 1973. P
       The activities of a German-born ex-professor
       who gets sent on secret missions by a President
       with bushy eyebrows: Curt Messinger resolves a
       monetary crisis with his computer brain and saves
       the life of Chou En-lai by outshooting four assassins
       in the Chinese premier's private conference room.

533   Fast, Howard. The Assassin Who Gave Up His Gun.
       By E. V. Cunningham, pseud. New York: Morrow,
       1969.
       Richard Breckner is the top liquidator on the
       staff of "The Department," a secret international
       organization with its own plans for the world's fu-
       ture. He falls in love and this "new experience"
       proves to be his professional undoing.

534   Faur, Michael P., Jr. A Friendly Place to Die.
       New York: Signet, 1969. P
       The CIA must chance trusting an American re-
       turned from 13 years in the interior of Red China
       because only he can supply invaluable data needed
       to forestall a world-shaking Communist plot.

535   Feakes, G. J. Moonrakers and Mischief. New
       York: Washburn, 1962.
       A bit of a gay novel set in the English country-
       side and involving the failure of a secret weapons
       project.

536   Fergusson, Bernard E. Rare Adventure. New York:
       Rinehart, 1954.
       A Scotsman visits a North African island and
       finds himself in an uprising against its French ad-
       ministration.

537   Firth, Anthony. Tall, Balding, Thirty-Five. New
       York: Harper, 1967.
       An English professor arrives in Bavaria and is
       projected into an intelligence caper being jointly
       carried out by British, American, French, and
       Russian agents against the Chinese.

538   Fish, Robert L. Always Kill a Stranger. New

York: Berkley, 1967. P
José da Silva of Brazilian security must prevent an assassination during an OAS meeting.

539   Fisher, Norman. Walk at a Steady Pace. New York:
        Walker, 1972.
        When a Russian satellite crashes into Italy,
        all the various spies set out to recover its payload.

540   Fleming, Ian. Bonded Fleming. New York: Viking,
        1965.
        This James Bond omnibus contains the following
        novels (cited with annotations below): For Your
        Eyes Only, The Spy Who Loved Me, and Thunder-
        ball.

541   _____. Casino Royale. New York: Macmillan,
        1954.
        Secret agent 007 enters a gambling contest in
        a casino in the south of France with orders to de-
        feat the corrupt French Communist trade union of-
        ficial Le Chiffre at baccarat, thereby breaking the
        man's influence, power, and bankroll.
        This was the first of the following spy novels
        which were destined to become perhaps the most
        famous in all espionage literature. The hero,
        James Bond, was one of 10 secret British Intelli-
        gence agents licensed to kill--hence the double-zero
        identification--and received his orders from a spy-
        master known only as "M."
        While no 007 ever really existed, there was a
        World War II agent of such skill that upon meeting
        him, Mr. Fleming modeled Bond after him. This
        meeting with "Tricycle," who was then in Spain is
        related by the subject, Dusko Popov, in his mem-
        oirs Spy Counter-Spy (New York: Grosset & Dun-
        lap, 1974).
        One might further note that character names in
        these spy yarns are unique. None are more worthy
        of note than those created by Mr. Fleming for the
        girls and villains encountered by 007.

542   _____. Diamonds Are Forever. New York:
        Macmillan, 1965.
        A fabulously wealthy racketeer has been spirit-
        ing vast quantities of diamonds out of South Africa
        and "M" assigns 007 to look into this so-called

"Spangled Mob. " The trail leads from Amsterdam
to Los Angeles and Las Vegas, where it turns out
the mastermind behind these huge thefts is Bond's
old enemy, Ernst Blofeld. The evil genius and his
girlfriend, Tiffany Case, a girl as hard as the
hardest "rock," are utilizing the facilities of a
nutty casino operator named Willard Whyte to gather
in the stones and thereafter construct a powerful
laser satellite which can be orbited over Washington
and used to blackmail America into surrender.

543   _____. Dr. No. New York: Macmillan, 1958.
        When an agent's radio goes dead in the West
Indies, Bond is sent out to investigate. There he
comes up against a mad half-Chinese/half-German
scientist intent on halting American rocket flights
from Cape Canaveral.

544   _____. For Your Eyes Only. New York: Viking,
        1960.
        Five Bond novelettes, including "From a View
of a Kill," "For Your Eyes Only," "Quantum of
Solace," "Risico," and "The Hildebrand Rarity. "

545   _____. From Russia With Love. New York:
        Macmillan, 1957.
        S. P. E. C. T. R. E. (The Special Executive for
Counter-Intelligence, Terrorism, Revenge, and Ex-
tortion), the same group of nasties to which Dr. No
belonged, is headed by the evil Ernst Stavro Blofeld,
who in this tale decides that the Russian Lektor
cipher machine should be stolen, the blame placed
squarely on Britain, and then it should be sold back
to the Soviets at a huge profit. The ploy works
out like this: Russian Tatiana Romanova, an employee of the Soviet embassy in Istanbul, "agrees"
to defect bringing the Lektor along, if James Bond
will pick them up. The nasty's thinking is that he
can avenge Dr. No. by doing 007 slowly in. There
is action galore as our hero encounters all sorts of
nasties in Istanbul and on the Orient Express headed
out of town.

546   _____. Goldfinger. New York: Macmillan, 1960.
        Bond duels arch criminal Auric Goldfinger for
control of the U.S. gold reserves in Fort Knox.

547   _____. Gilt-Edged Bonds. New York: Macmillan,
           1961.
           Omnibus containing Casino Royale, Dr. No,
           and From Russia with Love.

548   _____. Live and Let Die. New York: Macmillan,
           1954.
           "M" assigns 007 to take out the world's most
           powerful criminal, "Mr. Big" of the imfamous
           S. M. E. R. S. H.

549   _____. The Man with the Golden Gun. New York:
           New American Library, 1965.
           Bond returns to London as a homicidally brain-
           washed stooge of the KGB. He is immediately
           taken in hand, rewashed, and sent on his merry
           way to hamstring, not help one of his mortal ene-
           mies, Francisco Scaramanga, whom he meets in
           deadly combat on the island of Jamaica.

550   _____. Moonraker. New York: Macmillan, 1956.
           007 must investigate the motives behind an
           enigmatic millionaire who is financing a new super
           rocket that could destroy the world.

551   _____. More Gilt-Edged Bonds. New York:
           Macmillan, 1965.
           Another anthology of novels, this one contains:
           Diamonds Are Forever, Live and Let Die, and
           Moonraker. It is probably not necessary to remind
           readers that all of the Fleming novels are in con-
           stant reissue by various paperback publishers.

552   _____. On Her Majesty's Secret Service. New
           York: New American Library, 1963.
           In the Alps, 007 matches wits with arch-villian
           Ernst Stavro Blofeld, architect of another atomic
           blackmail scheme.

553   _____. Octopussy. New York: New American
           Library, 1966.
           The three last James Bond short stories, re-
           printed from Playboy and Argosy under a single
           cover. Two are worthy of annotation here: Octo-
           pussy concerns the last hours of a secret service
           agent who has gone to seed in Jamaica on some
           ill-got Nazi gold; The Living Daylights tells how

Bond was sent to pick a sniper off the Berlin Wall.

554   _____. The Spy Who Loved Me. New York:
           Viking, 1962.
           This is probably the least known, least favor-
           ably reviewed, and "different" of the Bond novels:
           Vivienne Michel's first-person account of a night of
           terror in the Dreamy Pines Motor Court in the
           Adirondacks as she shared it with James Bond, 007.

555   _____. Thunderball. New York: Macmillan, 1961.
           Bond destroys the attempt of arch criminal
           Blofeld to hold the world to ransom with a pair of nu-
           clear bombs stolen from a British bomber he caused
           to crash into the sea off the West Indies.

556   _____. You Only Live Twice. New York: New
           American Library, 1964.
           Bond arrives in Japan to take on Dr. Guntrum
           Shatterhand, who has set up a suicide park on a
           volcanic island and in the process meets his old
           enemy, Ernst Blofeld.

557   Fleming, Joan. When I Grow Rich. New York:
           Washburn, 1962. Y*
           A novel of suspense and intrigue set in Istanbul
           and involving a young Turkish philosopher, a teen-
           aged English girl, and an elderly harem woman.

558   Fletcher, Lucille. Blindfold. New York: Random
           House, 1960.
           New York psychiatrist Dr. Snow is asked by
           the CIA to treat a neurotic scientist.

559   Forbes, Colin. The Heights of Zervos. New York:
           Dutton, 1970. Y*
           This author ranks with Alistair MacLean (q.v.)
           as the master of clandestine commando tales. A
           British agent and three patriots must prevent the
           crack Alpenkorps from taking the monestary atop
           Mount Zervos in 1940 Greece.

560   _____. The Palermos Affair. New York: Dutton,
           1972. Y*
           Two Allied saboteurs employing local Mafia
           strongmen are involved in a race to sink a huge
           train-ferry between Sicily and the mainland of Italy

before the Germans can get panzer divisions across.

561 _____. Target Five. New York: Dutton, 1973. Y*
A Russian scientist with vital data makes a run
for freedom across the Arctic icepack. U.S. and
Soviet intelligence agents employing everything from
helicopters to icebreakers race to secure his person.

562 _____. Year of the Golden Ape. New York:
Dutton, 1974. Y*
Sheik Tafak plans to steal a British oil tanker,
put a nuclear bomb aboard, and blow up San Fran-
cisco with it. The anti-Arab outcry sure to follow
can then be used as an excuse to cut off all oil to
the West until Israel is abandoned by her capitalist
allies. Pitted against this mad caper is a lone
British intelligence agent.

563 Forrest, David. And to My Nephew Albert I Leave
the Island What I Won Off Fatty Hagan in a Poker
Game. New York: Morrow, 1969. H
One of--if not the--most humorous "spy" stories
ever written, this tale concerns a little speck of
land (70 x 150 yds.) off the coast of England. When
Albert takes over, he discovers the frequent presence of Victoria, who loves to sunbathe. Just as
the two are getting to know one another, a Soviet
spy trawler runs aground nearby--and about an hour
later, the U.S. Marines start landing....

564 _____. One of Our Dinosaurs Is Missing. New
York: Avon, 1975.
A Disneyish tale of five British nannys swiping
bones from an American museum containing a secret
microdot.

565 Forrester, Larry. A Girl Called Fathom. London:
Heinemann, 1967.
Douglas Campbell, head of NATO Intelligence,
abducts amateur spy Fathom Harvill and persuades
her to help find "The Fire Dragon," a nuclear
trigger device lost when a bomber crashed in the
Mediterranean.

566 Forsyth, Frederick. The Day of the Jackal. New
York: Viking, 1971.
By the spring of 1963, the right-wing OAS in

France, infuriated by General de Gaulle's with-
drawal from Algeria, had failed in six known assassination attempts on Le Grande Charles. Now they
sought to hire an outsider, a professional killer who
would be unknown to French police and intelligence.
In Vienna, a blond-haired Englishman takes on the
job. His code name: Jackal; his price: $500,000;
his demand: total secrecy, even from his employers.

567 _____. The Dogs of War. New York: Viking,
1974.
A London financial wizard and an Irish mercenary plot the takeover of Zangaro, a small west
African dictatorship with a secret source of platinum.

568 _____. The Odessa File. New York: Viking,
1972.
In the literature of intrigue and espionage,
"Odessa" is a group set up to protect former Nazi
SS officers now living under new identities. This
same organization is encountered in some of the
other stories cited in this compilation. Forsyth's
account is by and large the most gripping of the
Odessa tales and concerns a young German reporter,
Peter Miller, who, having read about a particularly
imfamous Nazi death camp, attempts to penetrate
Odessa to find its commandant, one Eduard Roschmann. Roschmann is alive and well and as one of
Odessa's top leaders, is up to his eyebrows in the
Arab missile program. He orders his confederates
to stop Miller before anything damaging can be
learned. A movie version has been released.

569 Fournier, Pierre. Lambs of Fire. By Pierre
Gascan, pseud. Transl. from French by Merloyd
Laurence. New York: Braziller, 1963.
A number of French "organization" men obtain
explosives to get back at the de Gaulle government
for "betraying" the army in Algeria. Written along
the lines of The Day of the Jackal.

Fox, James M., pseud. see Knipcheer, James M.

570 Francis, Richard. Blood Sport. New York: Harper,
1967.
On vacation from "The Agency," Gene Hawkins
decides to use his "talents" to help a friend recover

his precious racehorse, the third to recently dis-
appear. As much a detective as a spy story.

571 Frank, Patrick. Forbidden Area. Philadelphia:
Lippincott, 1956.
A suspenseful account of how a Russian plot to
annihilate America in the near future is broken up
by a few dedicated people.

572 Frayn, Michael. The Russian Interpreter. New
York: Viking, 1967.
A British graduate student at Moscow University
is bored. Then one snowy day, a shadowy industrial
magnate shows up and engages him as his interpreter.

573 Frazer, Steve. The Sky Block. New York: Rinehart,
1953. *
A country lad aids agents in their search for
the "Weather Wrecker," a machine causing drought
over wide areas.

574 Frede, Richard. The Coming Out Party. New York:
Random House, 1969.
When he goes on assignment for the CIA to a
Writers' Association Conference to uncover some
nasties an author finds he is faced with losing either
his pen name or his life.

575 Fredman, John. The False Joanna. Indianapolis:
Bobbs-Merrill, 1971.
A lush of a spy is sent by his superiors in "The
Fourth Agency" to find a girl which the KGB has
succeeded in smuggling into Britain.

576 _____. The Fourth Agency. Indianapolis: Bobbs-
Merrill, 1960.
Our alcoholic operative is ordered to commence
a dialogue with the GRU. The talks take place between Las Vegas and Mexico and are replete with
unusual implications.

577 Freedgood, Morton. Man in Question. By John
Godey, pseud. Garden City, N.Y.: Doubleday,
1951. *
Peter Manning comes to America from behind
the Iron Curtain to help in the anti-Communist

67 FREELING

resistance and is nearly done in. Not a bad
McCarthy era yarn.

578   Freeling, Nicholas. The Dresden Green. New York:
Harper, 1968.
The senior French-Russian translator at Euro-
paus, an organization devoted to peace and brother-
hood, finds a strange diamond--the Dresden Green--
under a quince tree. His discovery forces him to
resume the role he played twenty years earlier in
the French underground.

579   Freemantle, Brian. Goodbye to an Old Friend. New
York: Putnam, 1973.
A top Russian space scientist decides to defect,
leaving his family to possible reprisal. The Americans want to put Pavel to work immediately but
Adrian Dodds believes the man may be a plant and
sets out to prove his suspicions.

580   French, Richard P. A Spy Is Forever. Rutland, Vt.:
Tuttle, 1970.
Peter Layton must kill a National Intelligence
Agency colleague who has defected--only first he
must be found.

581   Frizell, Bernard. Ten Days in August. New York:
Simon & Schuster, 1957.
The German occupiers of Paris and the French
Resistance prepare for the Allied Liberation due any
moment.

582   Gadney, Reginald. Drawn Blanc. New York: Coward-
McCann, 1971.
Czech refugee O. B. Blanc will be forced to
return home where authorities want him for killing
a KGB man during the 1968 "unpleasantness";
British Intelligence steps in and makes an offer: if
Blanc will do a little job for them, his visa will be
extended.

583   Gainham, Sarah. Appointment in Vienna. New York:
Dutton, 1958.
A British agent is assigned to track down one
Otto Berger, who is rumored to have escaped

Hitler's bunker during the last days of the Reich
with a fortune in gold.

584 _____. Maculan's Daughter. New York: Putnam,
1974.
A British businessman marries the boss's
daughter to get at military secrets. When he dies,
his records raise sufficient doubt that an agent
posing as the company lawyer is called upon to
unravel the threads of treason. Other Gainham
suspense stories include:

585 _____. Cold Dark Night. New York: Dutton,
1958.

586 _____. Place in the Country. New York: Putnam,
1969.

587 _____. The Silent Hostage. New York: Dutton,
1961.
Mystery and intrigue in Modern Yugoslavia.

588 _____. Stone Roses. New York: Dutton, 1959.

589 _____. Time Right Deadly. New York: Dutton,
1956.

590 Gallery, Daniel J. The Brink. Garden City, N. Y.:
Doubleday, 1968.
In the Arctic an American nuclear submarine
confronts a Russian destroyer and World War III is
at the brink. Compare with Rascovich (1330).

591 Gallico, Paul. The Hand of Mary Constable. Garden
City, N. Y.: Doubleday, 1964.
Alexander Hero of the (British) Psychical Research Society is called upon to prevent Professor
Constable from turning over to the Russians the
secrets of a new missile defense system. The
Soviets, not to be outdone, produce a wax hand
bearing the fingerprints of the scientist's missing
daughter and promise her safe return in exchange
for his expert knowledge.

592 _____. Trial by Terror. New York: Knopf, 1952.
An American reporter purposefully delivers himself into the hands of Communist agents behind the
Iron Curtain to discover why a group of men con-
fessed to crimes they did not commit.

593 _____. The Zoo Gang. New York: Coward-
McCann, 1971. H
In this funny espionage-detective tale, a gang
of former Resistance fighters turn their talents to
halting the assorted crimes taking place on the
glamorous Riviera.

594 Gardner, Alan. Six Day Week. New York: Coward-
McCann, 1966.
Chinese Communists are working with Italian
Communists to kill a visiting British princess and
the Pope when they dedicate a new orphanage.

595 Gardner, John. Amber Nine. New York: Viking,
1966. H
Agent Brian I. "Boysie" Oakes is ordered to
assassinate a Member of Parliament at a quiet resort hotel on Lake Maggiore. The secret behind
the author's Oakes series is that his agent--the
official murderer of the Department of Special Security charged with removing individuals who become
embarrassing to the crown--never kills and is even
afraid of riding in airplanes. A charming bit of
British parody on the James Bond craze. Other
Oakes titles are:

596 _____. Air Apparent. New York: Viking, 1970.

597 _____. The Liquidator. New York: Viking,
1965. H

598 _____. Madrigal. New York: Viking, 1967. H
The dangers of Red Chinese agents and "co-
operating" with the KGB.

599 _____. Understrike. New York: Viking, 1965. H
San Diego, a hush-hush submarine trial, and a
carefully trained Russian double.

600 Garfield, Brian. Deep Cover. New York: Delacorte,
1973.
For over twenty years, Russians trained to "be
Americans" by the KGB, have been settling around
an Arizona missile base. One day the head of
Soviet Intelligence decides to put his long-awaited
operating involving these folks into high gear.

601 _____. Hopscotch. Philadelphia: Lippincott, 1975.
A CIA man no longer wants to caper, but

neither does he want to defect. Instead, he brings
the international intelligence community to a stand-
still by writing an expose. Aghast, agents from
all over the world gang up to do him in before he
can mail back to his publisher the final batch of
"proof."

602 _____. Kolchak's Gold. New York: McKay, 1973.
Five hundred tons of gold, hidden by the Whites
after the Russian Civil War, was stolen by the
Nazis and is now wanted by agents of the Soviet and
Western governments.

603 _____. Line of Succession. New York: Delacorte,
1972. *
In this part political, part espionage tale, an
"F.S.S." agent must get back to Washington with
the new President for swearing in ceremonies.

604 _____. The Romanov Succession. New York:
Evans, 1974. *
A White Russian is released from duty with the
U.S. Army and with the tacit consent of the Allied
governments, plots to overthrow Stalin, put a puppet prince in power, and wipe out the Communists.
A nice idea, this story is based on the fortunes of
a real life Soviet general, Andrew Vlasov, who
fought for the Germans against his countrymen and
was hanged by the Stalin regime shortly after V-E
Day.

605 Garforth, John. The Floating Game. New York:
Signet, 1967. P
During the middle 1960's, a highly popular
British import TV series was "The Avengers,"
which featured derby-and-cane John Steed, who
fancied old cars, and the glamorous Mrs. Peel,
adicted to sports cars and mod clothes. These
two battled all sorts of nasties to the delight of
English and American audiences every week.
These four titles are spin-offs from that series:

606 _____. The Laugh Was on Lazarus. New York:
Signet, 1967. P

607 _____. The Passing of Gloria Munday. New York:
Signet, 1967. P

608   _____. Heil Harris! New York: Signet, 1967. P

609   Garland, Rodney. Troubled Midnight. New York:
       Coward-McCann, 1955.
           A thinly disguised fictional account of the real-
       life defecting British diplomats, Donald MacLean
       and Guy Burgess. Liberally sprinkled with "gay"
       references.

610   Garner, William. The Deep, Deep Freeze. New
       York: Putnam, 1968.
           Mike Jagger is forced out of retirement to help
       an East German defect and expose a double agent in
       the pay of British Intelligence.

611   _____. Overkill. New York: New American Li-
       brary, 1966.
           Unemployed, Jagger uncovers a plot against
       international peace and works alone to undo it.

612   _____. The Us or Them War. New York: Put-
       nam, 1969.
           When a naive scientist succeeds in crossing an
       X-ray with a laser beam, Jagger is called upon to
       protect Britain's interest.

613   Garth, David. Three Roads to a Star. New York:
       . Putnam, 1955.

614   _____. Tortured Angel. New York: Putnam,
       1948.
           An ex-American officer is detailed by the State
       Department to track down some missing documents
       vital to peace.

       Garve, Andrew, pseud. see Winterton, Paul

615   Garvin, Richard M. and Edmond G. Addeo. The
       Fortec Conspiracy. Los Angeles: Sherbourne
       Press, 1968.
           When the U.S. Air Force buries Barney Russom's
       twin brother in a locked coffin and when they pay
       Bob's widow full insurance benefits, Barney decides
       to find out why. His search leads him to a small
       building at Wright Patterson AFB labeled simply
       Foreign Technology--FORTEC. Inside are....

Gascar, Pierre, pseud. see Fournier, Pierre

616 Gaskin, Catherine. The File on Devlin. Garden City, N.Y.: Doubleday, 1965.
A Nobel Peace Prize winner is thought to have defected and a British agent carries the investigation to a grim Swiss chateau.

617 Gates, Natalie. Hush, Hush Johnson. New York: Holt, 1969. H
In this spy spoof, plump British secretary is duped into smuggling some secret code-tapes.

618 George, Jonathan. The Kill Dog. Garden City, N.Y.: Doubleday, 1970.
Prague during the 1968 Soviet invasion: a professor and a English businesswoman seek to solve the riddle posed by a mysterious map.

619 Gibbs, Henry. Assassin's Road. By Simon Harvester, pseud. New York: Walker, 1966.
Secret agent Dorian Silk is in Jerusalem to discover the identity of "The Prophet" and to prevent his revival of the ancient sect known as "The Assassins." If he fails, this gang will stir up so much mischief in the Israeli countryside as to start a jihad, or "Holy War."

620 _____. The Bamboo Screen. By Simon Harvester, pseud. New York: Walker, 1969.
British hydroelectric expert U.S. enemy agents in Taiwan.

621 _____. Battle Road. By Simon Harvester, pseud. New York: Walker, 1967.
Agent Silk is ordered to Bangkok after a body is found in the Mekong River near Saigon.

622 _____. The Chinese Hammer. By Simon Harvester, pseud. New York: Walker, 1961.
An English astronaut returning from space crashes in Chinese-occupied Tibet.

623 _____. The Flying Horse. By Simon Harvester, pseud. New York: Walker, 1964.
First published in England as Troika. British agent sent after a defector to North Korea.

624 _____. Forgotten Road. By Simon Harvester, pseud. New York: Walker, 1974.

Silk turns up with amnesia at a village on the Indian-Afghani border.

625 _____. Moscow Road. By Simon Harvester, pseud. New York: Walker, 1971.
With a crash course in computer salesmanship as a cover, Silk is rushed off to Moscow.

626 _____. Nameless Road. By Simon Harvester, pseud. New York: Walker, 1970.
Silk is sent to Inner Mongolia to eliminate COMPACIN.

626 _____. Red Road. By Simon Harvester, pseud. New York: Walker, 1964.
A desperate escape by Silk across the Soviet frontier from Samarkand.

627 _____. Sahara Road. By Simon Harvester, pseud. New York: Walker, 1972.
Disguished as an archaeologist, Silk is sent to Algeria.

628 _____. Silk Road. By Simon Harvester, pseud. New York: Walker, 1964.
Silk finds his identity has been betrayed.

630 _____. Tiger in the North. By Simon Harvester, pseud. New York: Walker, 1963.
Set in Rajpul, a (fictitious) border kingdom of India: intrigue and British oil prospectors.

631 _____. Treacherous Road. By Simon Harvester, pseud. New York: Walker, 1967.
Can Dorian Silk persuade a fellow spy not to defect? Here are some more "Simon Harvester" secret agent novels:

632 _____. Arrival in Suspicion. New York: Walker, 1953.

633 _____. Breastplate for Aaron. New York: Walker, 1949.

634 _____. Cat's Cradle. New York: Walker, 1952.

635 _____. Copper Butterfly. New York: Walker, 1957.
Action in Japan.

636 _____. Delay in Danger. New York: Walker, 1954.

637 _____. Dragon Road. New York: Walker, 1956.
Dorian Silk in Thailand and Burma.

638   _____. Epitaph for Lemmings. New York:
            Walker, 1943.

639   _____. Flight in Darkness. New York: Walker,
            1965.

640   _____. Golden Fear. New York: Walker, 1957.

641   _____. An Hour Before Zero. New York: Walker,
            1960.
            Action in South Vietnam.

642   _____. Lantern for Diogenes. New York: Walker,
            1947.

643   _____. Let Them Prey. New York: Walker, 1942.

644   _____. Lucifer at Sunset. New York: Walker,
            1959.

645   _____. Maybe a Trumpet. New York: Walker,
            1945.

646   _____. Moonstone Jungle. New York: Walker,
            1961.
            Dorian Silk in the Far East.

647   _____. Paradise Men. New York: Walker, 1956.
            Action in New Guinea.

648   _____. Shadows in a Hidden Land. New York:
            Walker, 1966.
            Dorian Silk in the Far East.

649   _____. Sheep May Safely Graze. New York:
            Walker, 1950.

650   _____. Spider's Web. New York: Walker, 1953.

651   _____. Unsung Road. New York: Walker, 1960.
            Dorian Silk in the Far East.

652   _____. Vessels May Carry Explosives. New
            York: Walker, 1951.

653   _____. Whatsoever Things Are True. New York:
            Walker, 1947.

654   _____. Witch Hunt. New York: Walker, 1951.

655   _____. The Yesterday Walkers. New York:
            Walker, 1958.
            Action in Malaya.

656   _____. Zion Road. New York: Walker, 1968.
            Dorian Silk.

657   Gibson, Frank E. Cloak and Doctor. New York:
       Exposition, 1974. H
         A CIA doctor has zany adventures with patients
       and plots in Washington and Europe.

658   Gifford, Thomas. Wind Chill Factor. New York:
       Putnam, 1975.
         A gigantic Nazi conspiracy is afoot with bases
       around the world seeking international power. Can
       a lone agent stop it in time?

659   Gilbert, Michael. After the Fine Weather. New
       York: Harper, 1963.
         A bishop is assassinated in a small Austrian
       province and an English eyewitness is sought by
       enemy agents.

660   _____. Game Without Rules. New York: Harper,
       1967. H
         Eleven short spy stories concerning Messrs.
       Calder and Behrens, a pair of middle-aged agents
       working for the External Branch of Britain's Joint
       Services Standing Intelligence Committee, special-
       izing in unorthodox methods.

661   Gilman, Dorothy. The Amazing Mrs. Pollifax.
       Garden City, N.Y.: Doubleday, 1970. H*
         In this sequel to The Unexpected Mrs. Pollifax
       cited below, Emily is sent to Turkey to aid in the
       escape of a famous double agent.

662   _____. The Elusive Mrs. Pollifax. Garden City,
       N.Y.: Doubleday, 1971. H*
         While ancient Emily is watching her garden
       grow, Carstairs and Bishop of the CIA are in a
       Harlem hotel room wondering who they can get to
       smuggle desperately-needed passports to their man
       trapped in Sofia.

663   _____. A Palm for Mrs. Pollifax. Garden City,
       N.Y.: Doubleday, 1973. H*
         Emily's mission is to check into a Swiss hotel
       and try to trace some stolen plutonium with a
       miniature Geiger counter.

664   _____. The Unexpected Mrs. Pollifax. Garden
       City, N.Y.: Doubleday, 1966. H*

In this first of the "Pollifax Series," lonely
widow Emily Pollifax, a lady in her sixties, is
tapped by the CIA for a simple but important
courier assignment. Unfortunately, the unpredict-
able heroine is kidnapped to Albania.

665 Glaskin, G. M. The Man Who Didn't Count. New
York: Dial Press, 1967.
Hunted in London by Russian agents who pre-
sume him to be a defected nuclear scientist, Morton
Thomas escapes to Amsterdam only to be found
once again.

666 Goddard, Harry. The Silent Force. New York:
Popular Library, 1971. P
An incredible group of secret agents is turned
loose on organized crime.

Godey, John, pseud. see Freedgood, Morton

667 Goldberg, Marshall. Karamanov Equations. Cleveland: World, 1972.
Russian scientist, about to discover how to put
his nation ahead in the missile race, is suddenly
stricken and the best man for the surgery needed
is an American. The Russians send their man to
Paris where they hope to convince the Yanks he is
an unimportant Frenchman; the CIA is on top of
the game....

668 Goldman, James. Waldorf. New York: Random
House, 1966. H
In a forgotten village in Costa Rica, agents of
five nations are busy attempting to snitch a fugitive
Latin dictator. Waldorf Appleton, a painter and the
only non-affiliated male in town is mistaken for the
quarry.

669 Goodfield, June. Courier to Peking. New York:
Dutton, 1973.
The President of the National Academy of
Sciences visits Red China in the summer of 1971;
on the sly, he bears an important message.

670 Goodman, George J. W. and Winthrop Knowlton. A
Killing in the Market. Garden City, N. Y. : Doubleday, 1958.

In this cross between a mystery and a secret
agent tale, a Wall Street broker, ensnared unwit-
tingly into buying shares in a missile corporation
for an unknown European client, is held to the deal
by the kidnapping of his daughter.

671   Gordon, Alexander. The Cipher. New York: Simon
      & Schuster, 1962.
      An expert at cuneiform deciphers a diplomatic
      message from a Mideast nation to earn a little cash
      on the side. He is soon in great danger from a
      sinister international gang.

672   Gordon, Mildred and Gordon. Power Play. Garden
      City, N.Y.: Doubleday, 1965.
      A daring plot erupts to seize control of the FBI.

673   _____. Tiger on my Back. Garden City, N.Y.:
      Doubleday, 1960.
      American CIA girl drawn into a counter-spy
      deal in North Africa.

674   Grady, James. Shadow of the Condor. New York:
      Putnam, 1975.
      The further adventures of the hero of Six Days
      of the Condor.

675   _____. Six Days of the Condor. New York:
      Norton, 1974.
      A lowly CIA worker is propelled into a world
      of double agents and hired killers as his department
      is destroyed by "The Agency" itself.

676   _____. A Game for Heroes. Garden City, N.Y.:
      Doubleday, 1970.
      A one-eyed adventurer, spy, and daredevil
      commandos in a daring raid to take out a fortress
      the Germans have constructed on one of the Channel
      Islands. An enjoyable story, but no MacLean.

677   Graham, James. The Run to Morning. New York:
      Stein & Day, 1974.
      Adventurer Grant is blackmailed into breaking
      a gangster's grandson from an almost impregnable
      Libyan fortress where he has been interned. Action
      reminiscent of MacLean's Where Eagles Dare.

678   Graham, Winston. Night Journey. Garden City, N. Y.:
        Doubleday, 1968. *Y
             When the formula for a new kind of poison gas
        falls into the hands of a Nazi agent, British Intelli-
        gence determines to stop his dash back to Berlin--
        even if it means sacrificing a beautiful American
        agent and a brilliant British scientist to do it.

679   Graves, Richard L. The Black Gold of Malaverde.
        New York: Stein & Day, 1973.
             A bereaved father hires Wolfram, a demolitions
        expert, and his international gang to rub out a South
        American country where his son was brutally mur-
        dered.

680   _____. Cobalt 60. New York: Stein & Day, 1975.
             Before an Arab terrorist group can spread
        death in Washington, a multinational underground
        security agency moves to destroy its impregnable
        Red Sea island base.

681   _____. The Platinum Bullet. New York: Stein &
        Day, 1974.
             American forces plan to frustrate plans by
        schemer DePrundis to corner the international
        platinum market for Russia.

682   Green, Frederick L. Ambush for a Hunter. New
        York: Random House, 1953.
             What happens when a lovely but false Czech
        refugee arrives in England to effect the undoing of
        a noted chemist, is given shelter by Charles, a
        middleclass businessman on the way up, and is
        discovered by Edna, the Englishman's wife?

683   Greene, Graham. Ministry of Fear. New York:
        Viking, 1943. *
             Greene is a contemporary of Eric Ambler and
        is nearly as well known in the spy literature.
        Neither gentleman can be said to write spy stories
        as many of us understand them: rock-and-sock- 'em
        James Bond. Rather their penmanship leans strongly
        towards intrigue usually with just enough violence to
        make the story stand up.
             In this tale, we view the attempts of a group of
        pro-Nazi Englishmen to corner and murder a

neurotic Englishman who possesses a piece of military intelligence they want to pass on to Berlin.

684   _____. Our Man in Havana. New York: Viking,
          1958. *Y
          An Englishman accepts a secret agent post in
          Cuba with no intention of actually doing "the job."
          When the silly reports on guerrilla successes he has
          been sending to London start turning out to be true,
          he is precipitated into a rather nasty intrigue.

685   _____. The Quiet American. New York: Viking,
          1955. *Y
          Alden Pyle, sublimely innocent of intrigue and
          espionage except for what he was able to read in
          books, accompanies a British journalist to French
          Indo-China, during that earlier war with the Viet-
          Minh, on a secret mission for the State Department.

686   _____. The Third Man. New York: Viking,
          1950. *
          A relentless manhunt through postwar Vienna
          after one Harry Lime, supposed witness to a brutal
          murder. As much a mystery tale as an espionage
          caper, this work, an award-winning motion picture,
          can be held up as a good example of both.

687   Greene, Harris. The Flags at Doney. Garden City,
          N.Y.: Doubleday, 1964.
          In the spring of 1944, a band of Italian partisans,
          led by an American demolitions expert, is dispatched
          to destroy a railway bridge beyond Arpegno--a key
          German route. Can be compared with MacLean's
          The Guns of Navarone.

688   _____. The "Mozart" Leaves at Nine. Garden
          City, N.Y.: Doubleday, 1960.
          The U.S. Army Security Chief in 1946 Vienna
          is kept hopping as he hunts down left-over Nazis
          and Soviet agents.

689   _____. The Thieves of Tumbutu. Garden City,
          N.Y.: Doubleday, 1968.
          A small African sheikdom is suddenly brought
          into the 20th century with spies and intrigue every-
          where.

690   Greenlee, Sam.   The Spook Who Sat by the Door.
       New York: Dutton, 1969.
           Dan Freeman, the first Black CIA man, at-
       tempts to organize a Chicago ghetto gang into a
       guerrilla band.

       Griswold, George, pseud.   see   Dean, Robert G.

691   Guenter, C. H.   Max Galan #1: Hunter of Men.
       New York: Pinnacle Books, 1975.
           First of a new paperback series in which West
       German agent Max must return some stolen NATO
       secrets.

692   Gulyashki, Andrei.   The Zakhov Mission.   Transl. by
       Maurice Michael.   Garden City, N.Y.:   Doubleday,
       1969.
           This Bulgarian spy story concerns a Balkan
       agent assigned to find a top secret plan which has
       been stolen from the official Geological Survey and
       which shows the location of strategic minerals in
       an area not far from the border of a hostile
       country.

693   Gutteridge, Lindsay.   Cold War in a Country Garden.
       New York: Putnam, 1972.
           This is sort of a cross between "Land of the
       Lost" and "Mission Impossible." A British scien-
       tific experiment shrinks a group of secret agents
       down to 1/4" in size and then Intelligence employs
       them in the espionage game in a big way.

694   _____.   Killer Pine. New York: Putnam, 1973.
           One of the little operatives shrunk above un-
       covers a bizarre plot engineered by a Russian
       mastermind in the wilderness of the Rocky Moun-
       tains.

       Habe, Hans, pseud.   see   Bekessy, Jean

       Haggard, William, pseud.   see   Clayton, Richard

695   Haig, Alec.   Sign on for Tokyo.   New York: Dodd,
       Mead, 1969.
           The author "reveals" his role as an industrial

spy for Instecon Steel, who finds that he must cross
swords with his counterpart from Japan's Mitziguichi
Steel over a stolen British process for making phos-
phorous-free metal.

Haim, Victor, coauthor see Vicas, Victor

Hall, Adam, pseud. see Trevor, Elleston

696   Hall, Andrew. Frost. New York: Putnam, 1967.
      Thomas H. Stern returns home every Friday
from his London civil service job to his house in
Essex. This Friday, however, spies kidnap him.

697   Hall, Patrick. The Power Sellers. New York: Put-
      nam, 1969.
      The Buro Fletzer is an international armaments
syndicate operating out of Zurich and dedicated to
death in any spot on Earth. The more secret agent
Griffiths becomes involved with it, the more he
wants out.

698   Hall, Roger. 19. New York: Norton, 1970.
      Colonel Jabez Sparhawk sets up 19, an anony-
mous unofficial counterespionage group that operates
within the official intelligence apparatus and is designed solely to safeguard it from penetration in
this country. Soon its agents are on the track of
a sick patient who has escaped from the CIA's funny
farm.

699   Hamilton, Adam. The Yashar Pursuit. New York:
      Berkeley, 1974. P
      Agent Barrington Hewes-Bradford, "the Peace-
maker," seeks out those who have stolen some
dangerous nerve gas. Two other tales in "The
Peacemaker" series are:

700   _____. The Xander Pursuit. New York: Berkley,
      1974. P

701   _____. The Zaharan Pursuit. New York:
      Berkley, 1974. P

702   Hamilton, Donald. The Ambushers. Greenwich,
      Conn.: Fawcett, 1963. P
      Agent Matt Helm works his way from an assas-
sination in Costa Verde to the pursuit of an ex-Nazi

into northern Mexico. This Matt Helm series, like the Sam Durell and Nick Carter, is another of those paperback spy-adventure entries which have received mass attention.

703 _____. Assassins Have Starry Eyes. Greenwich, Conn.: Fawcett, 1973. P

704 _____. The Betrayers. Greenwich, Conn.: Fawcett, 1971. P

705 _____. Death of a Citizen. Greenwich, Conn.: Fawcett, 1972. P

706 _____. The Deceivers. Greenwich, Conn.: Fawcett, 1972. P

707 _____. The Devastators. Greenwich, Conn.: Fawcett, 1973. P
Scottish mad scientist plots world epidemic of bubonic plague.

708 _____. The Interlopers. Greenwich, Conn.: Fawcett, 1972. P
Helm takes over another man's identity, fiancée, and fate in a desperate attempt to decoy a Presidential assassin's dream.

709 _____. The Intimidators. Greenwich, Conn.: Fawcett, 1974. P
Caribbean rebels hijack American planes and ships.

710 _____. The Intriguers. Greenwich, Conn.: Fawcett, 1973. P
Helm must protect his top secret agency, I.C.E., from a political manipulator.

711 _____. Mad River. Greenwich, Conn.: Fawcett, 1974. P

712 _____. The Menacers. Greenwich, Conn.: Fawcett, 1973. P

713 _____. Murderers Row. Greenwich, Conn.: Fawcett, 1974. P
To destroy Washington, a scientist is kidnapped to force him to reveal the secrets of the Helio-Beam. Matt Helm jogs between the Riviera and America to quash plan, save scientist and woo daughter.

714 _____. Night Walker. Greenwich, Conn.: Fawcett, 1973. P

715   _____. The Poisoners. Greenwich, Conn.: Faw-
           cett, 1971. P
           Helm is ordered to California to foil the evil
           Warfel, who is planning to smuggle dope into
           America.

716   _____. The Ravagers. Greenwich, Conn.: Faw-
           cett, 1972. P

717   _____. The Removers. Greenwich, Conn.: Faw-
           cett, 1970. P

718   _____. The Shadowers. Greenwich, Conn.: Faw-
           cett, 1972. P
           Helm assumes the identity of a missing man
           as cover to foil a nasty plot and fools everyone
           except the man's wife. Similar to The Interlopers
           (708).

719   _____. The Silencers. Greenwich, Conn.: Faw-
           cett, 1973. P
           "Big O," a criminal Far Eastern organization
           is planning to divert missiles fired from New Mex-
           ico and cause widespread destruction.

720   _____. The Terminators. Greenwich, Conn.:
           Fawcett, 1975. P
           The latest available Matt Helm adventure.

721   _____. The Wrecking Crew. Greenwich, Conn.:
           Fawcett, 1970. P
           To spread financial chaos throughout the West,
           the deadly Count Contini hijacks $1 billion in gold
           bullion in Denmark. I.C.E. sends in Helm....

722   Hammond-Innes, Ralph. Attack Alarm. By Hammond
           Innes, pseud. New York: Macmillan, 1942. Y*
           A Nazi spy group attempts to cripple the RAF
           during the Battle of Britain.

723   _____. Blue Ice. By Hammond Innes, pseud.
           New York: Harper, 1949. Y*
           A wild chase after a fugitive possessing secrets
           is carried on by yacht and overland into the rugged
           mountains of Norway.

724   Hardt, Michael. Stranger and Afraid. Indianapolis:
           Bobbs-Merrill, 1943. Y*
           An Austrian passes vital data out of wartime
           Vienna to U.S. Army Intelligence.

725 Hardy, Ronald. The Face of Jalanath. New York:
Putnam, 1973.
Six men are chosen and trained to climb a peak
between Kashmir and China to take out China's nuclear potential.

726 Harling, Robert. Endless Colonnade. New York:
Putnam, 1960.
Dr. Rupert Frost finds himself in possession
of H-bomb secrets one of his colleagues was about
to turn over the Communists in Italy.

727 _____. The Enormous Shadow. New York:
Harper, 1955.
A London reporter works to expose a British
Member of Parliament and a big-name mathemati-
cian as members of a Communist spy ring.

728 Harper, Richard J. The Dragonhead Deal. New
York: Warner Paperback Library, 1975.
Employing a converted U-boat, Israeli spies
attempt to safeguard an illegal arms shipment.

729 Harrington, William. The Jupiter Crisis. New
York: McKay, 1971.
A reporter risks his life to follow a trail that
leads across Europe from a Soviet-captured U.S.
spy satellite to Washington and the President himself.

730 Harris, Tom. Black Sunday. New York: Putnam,
1975.
The Black September Palestine terrorist movement employs a disgruntled American blimp commander in a mad scheme to drop a huge anti-per-
sonnel bomb on the Super Bowl, killing the U.S.
President and 80,000 spectators. Major Kabakov
of Israeli Intelligence must stop them.

731 Harrison, Harry. Queen Victoria's Revenge. Garden
City, N.Y.: Doubleday, 1975.
Skyjacking; Cuban, Scotch, and Palestinian
revolutionaries vs U.S., Israeli, and British agents.

732 Hartenfels, Jerome. Doctor Death. New York: Hill
& Wang, 1970.
A British bank clerk is recruited by a weird

group calling itself the Experimental Institute of
Psychocontrol headed by the mysterious Doctor
Death--an ex-Nazi scientist guilty of all sorts of
grisly war crimes.

Harvester, Simon, pseud. see Gibbs, Henry

733   Hawkins, John and Ward. Pilebuck. New York:
       Dutton, 1943.
       Nazi sabotage in an American shipyard.

734   Haycraft, Howard, ed. Five Great Spy Novels.
       Garden City, N.Y.: Doubleday, 1962. Y*
       Contains the following, several of which were
       penned before 1937 and therefore are not cited with
       annotations herein: The Great Impersonation, by
       E. P. Oppenheim; Greenmantle, by John Buchan;
       Epitaph for a Spy, by Eric Ambler; No Surrender,
       by Martha Albrand, pseud. ; and No Entry, by
       Manning Coles, pseud.

735   Hayes, Roy. The Hungarian Game. New York:
       Simon & Schuster, 1973.
       An American counterespionage agent seeks a
       colonel of the Hungarian secret police, long believed
       dead, who surfaces at a California ski resort with
       a group of Albanians bankrolled by a rich Californian.

736   Hebden, Mark. A Killer for the Chairman. New
       York: Harcourt, 1972.
       A part-Chinese British secret agent is sent
       after a deranged spy who hates the Chinese and
       plans to murder Mao Tse-tung.

737   _____. March of Violence. New York: Harcourt,
       1970.
       Two of 100,000 students who march on a Ger-
       man city are not interested in education; they have
       in mind blowing up a British missile base.

738   _____. A Pride of Dolphins. New York: Har-
       court, 1975.
       Someone wants ex-Navy men for an about-to-be-
       hijacked submarine and James Venner infiltrates
       the crew for Intelligence just as the Royal Navy dis-
       covers the sub in question is carrying dangerous
       nerve gas.

739   Heberden, Mary V.   Secrets for Sale.   By Charles L.
      Leonard, pseud.   Garden City, N. Y. :   Doubleday,
      1950.
            Paul Kilgerrin, a sardonic private eye, sallies
      forth to do battle with enemy agents.

740   .   Treachery in Trieste.   By Charles L.
      Leonard, pseud.   Garden City, N. Y. :   Doubleday,
      1951.
            Kilgerrin is once more caught up in international
      intrigue, this time in Yugoslavia.

741   Heckstall-Smith, Anthony.   The Man With Yellow
      Shoes.   New York: Roy, 1958.
            A middle-aged Englishman dresses himself up
      as an Arab to foil an Egyptian plot against the
      diminishing British interests in the Middle East.

742   Heim, Michael.   Aswan! New York: Knopf, 1972.
            In this thriller, an international effort is
      mounted to keep Egypt from being swept into the
      Mediterraean after the crumbling of the high dam
      at Aswan.   Did someone blow it?

743   Helitzer, Florence.   Hans, Who Goes There? New
      York: Harper, 1965.
            A German survivor of Dachau and underling in
      American Intelligence leads a rather comfortable
      life until the day his boss sends him back to his
      old hometown to ferret out ex-Nazi Siegfried Gomul,
      suspected of collusion with East German agents.

744   Henderson, James.   Copperhead. New York: Knopf,
      1971.
            Twelve people are infected with a new germ,
      but as they wander, they keep it under control with
      a special antidote carried on a penny, or "copper-
      head." When two go to Russia, the Soviets accuse
      the West of attempting biological warfare and their
      agents, plus the CIA, must locate the other ten to
      end the experiment--only they are missing.

745   Henissart, Paul.   Narrow Exit. New York: Simon &
      Schuster, 1974.
            The first time Arab militant Al Houaranni
      leaves the Mideast, Israeli Intelligence sends its
      top man, Alex Gauthier, to kidnap him.

746   Herron, Shaun. The Hound and the Fox and the Har-
       per. New York: Random House, 1970.
           Retired secret agent Miro wants to write a book
       exposing "The Firm" for which he worked until it
       betrayed him. Of course, his ex-employers take
       steps to see that his writings never see print--and
       the Russians take steps to see that they do!

747   _____. Miro. New York: Random House, 1969.
           Tough agent Miro then working for "The Firm"
       is sent to Canada to find out who is behind a rash
       of unique murders.

748   _____. Through the Dark and Hairy Wood. New
       York: Random House, 1972.
           Agent Miro, peacefully retired to a farm in
       Southern Ireland, runs up to Ulster for livestock;
       while there, he stays with a Protestant leader.
       When an attempt is made on his host's life, British
       Intelligence enlists Miro as his bodyguard.

749   Hesky, Olga. A Different Night. New York: Random
       House, 1971.
           Somebody wants to assassinate an American
       presidential assistant en route to a conference in
       Israel. A Jewish agent and the CIA must find out
       who.

750   _____. The Serpent's Smile. New York: Dodd,
       Mcad, 1967.
           Another look at operations by Israeli Intelligence.

751   _____. Time for Treason. New York: Dodd,
       Mcad, 1968.
           A body is found hanging on a Tel Aviv slaughter
       house and Papa Barzilai, head of the top secret
       Israeli agency G.A.G., must learn the connection
       between it and a fire in a secret laboratory of the
       Weitzmann Institute at Rehovot.

752   Higgins, Jack. The Eagle Has Landed. New
       York: Harper, 1975.
           German attempt to kidnap Churchill late in the
       war.

753   _____. East of Desolation. Garden City, N.Y.:
       Doubleday, 1969.

Bush pilot Joe Martin teams up with friends to
halt nefarious plot on the Greenland ice cap.

754   _____. The Savage Day. New York: Holt, 1972.
A gunrunner is sprung from a Greek prison by
British Intelligence on condition that he pose as an
undercover arms dealer to the I.R.A.

Highet, Helen see MacInnes, Helen

755   Highsmith, Patricia. Ripley's Game. New York:
Knopf, 1974.
American Tom Ripley plays a dangerous game
with the fate of a mild-mannered Englishman and
his French wife.

756   Hill, John.   The Man From U.N.C.L.E.'s ABC of
Espionage. New York: Signet, 1966. P*
A look at the "ways and means" of spying as
taken from the files of that famous TV organization.

757   Hirschfeld, Burt.   The Masters Affair. New York:
Arbor House, 1971.
The assassination of a top Washington intelli-
gence official starts off the action.

758   Hoffenberg, Jack.   A Thunder at Dawn. New York:
Dutton, 1965.
Agents Jim Gerard and Alec Fletcher with an
integrated American CIA cast attempt to prevent a
Castro-like takeover on the island of Liberté.

759   Hogstrand, Olle.   The Debt. New York: Pantheon,
1975.
The murder of an employee of Sweden's Psychological Defense Department throws suspicion on
three men.

760   _____. On the Prime Minister's Account. New
York: Pantheon, 1972.
A fanatical leftist has assassinated the American
ambassador to Sweden; in what appears to be re-
taliation, the daughter of the Swedish prime minister
is kidnapped and the world learns she will be released when the diplomat's killer is caught.

761   Holly, J. Hunter.   The Assassination Affair. New

York: Ace, 1967.   PH
    T. H. R. U. S. H. launches all-out war on
U. N. C. L. E. 's top enforcement agents--with Napoleon
Solo and Illya Kuryakin their first targets.
    The highly popular "Man from U. N. C. L. E." TV
series was a hallmark of the James Bond era and
spun off from it were two dozen exclusively
paperback adventures. All were published by
the New York firm of Ace Books between 1965
and 1968 and are listed here by author:

762   Avallone, Michael. The Thousand Coffins Affair.

763   Davies, Frederick. The Cross of Gold Affair.

764   Leslie, Peter. The Diving Dames Affair.

765   _____. The Finger in the Sky Affair.

766   _____. The Radioactive Camel Affair.

767   _____. The Splinter Sunglasses Affair.

768   _____. The Unfair Fare Affair.

769   McDaniel, David. The Dagger Affair.

770   _____. The Hollow Crown Affair.

771   _____. The Monster Wheel Affair.

772   _____. The Rainbow Affair.

773   _____. The Utopia Affair.

774   _____. The Vampire Affair.

775   Oram, John. The Copenhagen Affair.

776   _____. The Stone Cold Dead in the Market Affair.

777   Phillifent, John T. The Corfu Affair.

778   _____. The Mad Scientist Affair.

779   _____. The Power Cube Affair.

780   Stratton, Thomas. The Invisibility Affair.

781   _____. The Mind Twisters Affair.

782   Whittington, Harry. The Doomsday Affair.

783   Homewood, Harry. A Matter of Size. New York:
    O'Hara, 1975.

784   Hone, Joseph. The Private Sector. New York:
    Dutton, 1972.

The fortunes of several people of various de-
grees of dedication in British Intelligence are followed in London and Cairo.

785   _____. The Sixth Directorate. New York: Dutton,
           1975.
           A subversive group among Russian Intelligence
           agents.

786   Hostovsky, Egon. Midnight Patient. Translated from
           Czech by Philip H. Smith. New York: Appleton-
           Century, 1954.
           A Czech doctor in New York is approached by
           American agents and asked to restore the dangerous
           mission

787   Household, Geoffrey. Arabesque. Boston: Little,
           Brown, 1948.
           Not to be confused with the Gregory Peck movie
           based on Gordon Cotler's The Cipher. British In-
           telligence gives Armande Heine a new purpose in
           life as she drifts from Beirut to Jerusalem--an
           agent in the Palestine difficulties spying on Jew
           and Arab alike.

788   _____. Doom's Caravan. Boston: Little, Brown,
           1971.
           An English spy who can pass for an Arab de-
           serts British Intelligence during World War II and
           our narrator-hero catches up with him in Lebanon
           and forces the man to help forestall a Nazi plot to
           take over the entire Middle East.

789   _____. Fellow Passenger. Boston: Little,
           Brown, 1955. *
           Atomic scientists and secret agents are mixed
           up with a young Englishman returning home to
           claim his estate.

790   _____. High Place. Boston: Little, Brown,
           1950. *
           An English intelligence officer in Syria attempts
           to disperse a band of international anarchists.

791   _____. Olura. Boston: Little, Brown, 1965.
           British Intelligence at work in the Mideast.

792   _____. Red Anger. Boston: Little, Brown, 1975.
         A retired agent becomes mixed up with the
         CIA, KGB, and MI-5 as he seeks safety from false
         charges.

793   _____. Rogue Male. Boston: Little, Brown,
         1939. Y*
         Spotted aiming his rifle at the mountain terrace
         of a certain unnamed European dictator (Hitler),
         a wealthy English big game hunter is pursued
         across the Continent and back to Britain.

794   _____. A Rough Shoot. Boston: Little, Brown,
         1951. *
         Roger Taine aids a Polish patriot in foiling the
         attempt of a Fascist organization to take over
         Great Britain.

795   _____. A Time to Kill. Boston: Little, Brown,
         1951. *
         In this sequel to A Rough Shoot, Taine's chil-
         dren are kidnapped by Russian agents because he is
         raising the hue and cry against a scientist he be-
         lieves is planning biological mischief on England.

796   _____. Watcher in the Shadows. Boston: Little,
         Brown, 1960.
         During the war a Vietnamese served in British
         Intelligence as a double-agent appearing to be a
         Nazi; how in Asia he is pursued by a man still
         thinking that his cover as a German sympathizer
         was real.

797   Howard, Clark. Summit Kill. New York: Pinnacle
         Books, 1975. P
         A plot is afoot to assassinate the world's five
         most important leaders meeting "at the summit. "

798   Howard, Hartley. Department "K." London: Collins,
         1970.
         Philip Scott is a British toy maker who employs
         his frequent merchandizing trips to Germany as a
         cover for his espionage activities. Basis of the
         movie Assignment "K. "

799   Howe, George. Call It Treason. New York: Viking,
         1949.

Three German POW's in the pay of U.S. Army
Intelligence are parachuted as saboteurs into Nazi
Germany. The narrative follows their pre-mission
training and the progress of one of them through
part of the Reich. Sort of a scaled-down, one-
quarter Dirty Dozen.

800   Hubler, Richard G.   The Chase.   New York: Coward-
McCann, 1952.
Foreign and American spies, a mysterious mad
scientist, and an innocent girl reporter hot-footing
it through the mountains near the coast of California.

801   Hughes, Dorothy B.   The Blackbirder.   New York:
Duell, 1943.   *
A young refugee from occupied France leads
the FBI to enemy agents on the Mexican-U.S. border.

802   _____.   The Davidian Report.   New York: Duell,
1952.   *
The FBI, CCI, and Red agents are all interested in a strange scientific exposé.

803   Huie, William B.   In the House of Night.   New York:
Delacorte, 1975.
The circumstances surrounding a public ser-
vant's psychological collapse as they relate to government security in the age of atomic secrets.

804   Humes, H. L.   The Underground City.   New York:
Random House, 1958.
An American agent works with the French
Resistance and after the war becomes the center
of interest in the trial of an accused collaborator.

805   Hunt, E. Howard.   The Berlin Ending.   New York:
Putnam, 1973.
CIA agent Thorpe tries to save the daughter of
a treacherous West German foreign minister secretly in league with the Russians.

806   _____.   Diabolus.   By David St. John, pseud.   New
York: Weybright & Talley, 1971.
Vacationing in the Caribbean, CIA agent Peter
Ward is involved in voodoo and a Red Chinese plot
to take over the French islands of the West Indies.

Other Ward adventures are:

807   ————. Festival for Spies. By David St. John,
pseud. New York: Weybright & Talley, 1966.
A plot to pull Cambodia into the Chinese orbit.

808   ————. Give Us This Day. By David St. John,
pseud. New York: Signet, 1974. P

809   ————. I Came to Kill. New York: Signet,
1973. P

810   ————. Judas Hour. By David St. John, pseud.
New York: Signet, 1973. P

811   ————. Lovers Are Losers. By David St. John,
pseud. New York: Signet, 1973. P

812   ————. The Mongol Mask. By David St. John,
pseud. New York: Weybright & Talley, 1968.
The CIA has no reliable data on China's only
missile base and Ward is sent to Mongolia.

813   ————. On Hazardous Duty. By David St. John,
pseud. New York: Signet, 1960. P
Two men whose careers are at stake--dedicated
CIA agent Ward and a top Soviet scientist on the
verge of defecting.

814   ————. One of Our Agents Is Missing. By David
St. John, pseud. New York: Weybright & Talley,
1969.
To Tokyo to investigate the disappearance,
leads to the biggest sell-out in history.

815   ————. Return from Vorkuta. By David St. John,
pseud. New York: Weybright & Talley, 1965.
Sent behind the Iron Curtain.

816   ————. The Sorcerers. By David St. John, pseud.
New York: Weybright & Talley, 1970.
Russian attempt to spread Communism by cor-
rupting Black African students.

817   ————. Towers of Silence. By David St. John,
pseud. New York: Signet, 1966. P

818   ————. Venus Probe. By David St. John, pseud.
New York: Signet, 1966. P

819   ————. Whisper Her Name. By David St. John,
pseud. New York: Signet, 1973. P

820 Hunter, Jack D. The Expendable Spy. New York:
Dutton, 1965.
An intelligence agent is sent on a desperate
mission knowing that should he fail, his presence
will not be missed.

821 _____. One of Us Works for Them. New York:
Dutton, 1967.
One night a U. S. Army agent discovers a leak
in his outfit in Heidelberg and is assigned to plug
it by framing a fellow officer.

822 Hyland, Henry S. Green Grow the Tresses-O. Indianapolis: Bobbs-Merrill, 1959. H
A bit of a spoof involving the boys from MI5.

823 _____. Top Bloody Secret. Indianapolis: Bobbs-
Merrill, 1969.
As the result of the first murder in the House
of Commons since 1812 and the loss of vital atomic
secrets, the men of MI5 set forth on a dangerous
chase through Belgium, Germany, Greece, and
Turkey.

824 Iams, Jack. Into Thin Air. New York: Morrow,
1952. *
An official of the Voice of America is drawn
into an espionage plot.

825 _____. Shot for Murder. New York: Morrow,
1951. *
This is not a murder mystery but a story of
international intrigue set behind the Iron Curtain
in post-war Poland.

Innes, Hammond, pseud. see Hammond-Innes, Ralph

Innes, Michael, pseud. see Stewart, John I. M.

826 Irving, Clifford. The Thirty-Eighth Floor. New
York: McGraw-Hill, 1965.
Our hero is a Black American upon whose
shoulders suddenly falls the successful running of
the U. N. All John Burden has to do is follow his
conscience and avoid international complications.

Unfortunately, his race, the intrigues of various
nasties, and his Communist Chinese mistress all
gum up the works somewhat.

827   Jacks, Oliver. Man on a Short Leash. New York:
        Stein & Day, 1974.
              In a bit of the old double-cross, agent Todd is
        accused of being a traitor and sentenced to thirty
        years in prison. Is this a cover?

828   Jahn, Michael. The Six Million Dollar Man: Wine,
        Women and War. New York: Warner Paperback
        Library, 1975.
              The first of a series tied into the TV series,
        in turn based on the CYBORG titles by Caidin
        (nos. 206-212). Steve Austin is sent to the Ba-
        hamas to uncover a cache of stolen missiles.

829   James, Leigh. The Capitol Hill Affair. New York:
        Weybright & Talley, 1969.
              Ernie Sessens of the CIA must employ the ser-
        vices of reporter Tony Baylor to find out how and
        why important secrets are oozing out of Washington.

830   _____. The Chameleon File. New York: Wey-
        bright & Talley, 1969.

831   _____. The Push Button Spy. New York:
        Prentice-Hall, 1970.
              A CIA operative is deliberately "brainwashed"
        by his superiors to believe he is operating for the
        Russians, but fights to prevent his becoming an
        automaton--or push-button spy.

832   Jay, Geraldine. Arms for Adonis. By Charlotte
        Jay, pseud. New York: Harper, 1961.
              A story of intrigue in the Arab world as Sarah
        sees a bomb explode on a Beirut street and is im-
        mediately picked up by a handsome stranger who
        leads her through various thrilling episodes of
        derring-do.

833   Jay, Simon. Sleepers Can Kill. Garden City, N.Y.:
        Doubleday, 1968.
              Mike Conners of the secret New Zealand

intelligence agency known as "The Fisheries" must recover a stolen secret laser weapon before the Communists can employ it.

834 Jenkins, Geoffrey. Hunter-Killer. New York: Putnam, 1967.

An astronaut turned American Vice President and an agent of British Naval Intelligence collaborate to launch an Anglo-America missile despite opposition from a hunter-killer task force of the U.S. Seventh Fleet.

Other tales by this author include:

835 _____. Grue of Ice. New York: Putnam, 1962.

836 _____. River of Diamonds. New York: Putnam, 1964.

837 _____. Twist of Sand. New York: Putnam, 1959.

838 Jepson, Selwyn. The Assassin. Philadelphia: Lippincott, 1957.

Ex-Major John Farr is in the top secret British Service. His tranquility as a broker (his cover) is broken by murder, espionage, embezzlement, stock-manipulation, and adultery all related to one important, but difficult intelligence caper.

839 _____. A Noise in the Night. Philadelphia: Lippincott, 1957.

A mild-mannered Suffolk England bank manager sets out merely to save his daughter from marrying "the wrong man" and ends up saving civilization from World War III as plotted by Arab extremists.

840 John, Owen. Sabotage. New York: Dutton, 1973.

A Communist saboteur, passing as a contractor's technician, infiltrates the defenses of a nuclear power plant in Wales and plants a bomb in a tank of fuel on the conveyor that feeds the reactor. In London, Intelligence learns this fellow is on the loose.

841 _____. The Shadow in the Sea. New York: Dutton, 1972.

An unidentified submarine is lurking off the British coast awaiting a shipment to Israel scheduled to be made aboard the freighter Nijmegen. A half-

Russian secret agent is sent to the Soviet Union to
find out what's up--or rather, what is going down.
Other spy stories by this author include:

842   _____. Beam of Black Light. New York: Dutton,
           1968.

843   _____. Dead on Time. New York: Dutton, 1969.

844   _____. The Disinformer. New York: Dutton,
           1967.

845   _____. Thirty Days Hath September. New York:
           Dutton, 1966.

846   Johnson, James L. A Piece of the Moon Is Missing.
       Philadelphia: Lippincott, 1974.
           Operator Sebastian is pitted against ruthless
       enemy agents and the Arctic perils of wolves,
       frostbite, and snow blindness in an effort to re-
       cover a vital package.

847   Johnson, Uwe. Speculations About Jakob. Transl.
       by Ursule Molinaro. New York: Grove Press,
       1963.
           An East German railway worker falls in love
       with a NATO agent. The Intelligence bosses of the
       People's Republic are naturally upset about this
       and suspecting him of wanting to defect and her of
       some nasty mission, order their men out to keep
       a close watch.

848   Johnston, William. Get Smart. New York: Signet,
       1965. PHY*
           The bumbling agent Maxwell Smart and his fe-
       male helper, Agent 99, were a comedy stalwart of
       American TV during the James Bond era. Five
       other spinoffs were also written:

849   _____. Get Smart Once Again. New York: Signet,
           1966. PHY*

850   _____. And Loving It. New York: Signet,
           1967. PHY*

851   _____. Max Smart and the Perilous Pellets. New
           York: Signet, 1966. PHY*

852   _____. Missed by that Much! New York: Signet,
           1967. PHY*

853   _____. Sorry Chief! New York: Signet,
             1966. PHY*

854   Jones, Philip. The Month of the Pearl. New York:
          Holt, 1965.
             A battle of wits between a professional assassin
          and a British agent in Rome.

855   Jordan, David. Nile Green. New York: Stein &
          Day, 1974.
             Essentially a spy story, our tale concerns the
          twisting turns growing out of commercial rivalries
          between the British and the Russians with regard
          to development schemes in Egypt.

856   Jordan, Len. Operation Perfidia. New York: War-
          ner Paperback Library, 1975.
             Who is setting up an ex-CIA agent fresh out of
          prison?

857   Julitte, Pierre. Block 26: Sabotage at Buchenwald.
          Trans. from French by Francis Price. Garden
          City, N.Y.: Doubleday, 1971. *
             Outside the infamous death camp where a num-
          ber of French Resistance workers are housed, the
          Germans have a secret plant where several are
          employed. When they discover that the project is
          building components for the V-2 missile, they plot
          to blow up "the factory."

858   Kagley, Rudolf. The Imposter. By Kurt Steel,
          pseud. New York: Harcourt, 1942. Y*
             Nazi saboteurs attack U.S. aircraft production.

859   Kane, Henry. Conceal and Disguise. By Anthony
          McCall, pseud. New York: Macmillan, 1967.
             Inspector McGregor is hired back by his old
          firm, the CIA, to evaluate a potential assassin.

860   _____. Holocaust. By Anthony McCall, pseud.
          New York: Macmillan, 1967.
             McGregor does his utmost to prevent it.

861   _____. Laughter in the Alehouse. By Anthony
          McCall, pseud. New York: Macmillan, 1968.

A beautiful Israeli agent entices McGregor into
a deadly Manhattan manhunt for a Nazi war criminal-
at-large.

862   _____. Operation Delta. By Anthony McCall,
       pseud. New York: Simon and Schuster, 1967.
           Tragedy strikes the four men responsible for a
       new missile project. Chris Adams, head of his own
       Adams Associates, must find the faceless enemy re-
       sponsible for mucking up his firm's project.

863   Katcher, Leo. The Blind Cave. New York: Viking,
       1966.
           American agent Richard Landon leads his col-
       leagues from Britain and the U.S., as well as
       Russia and Greece, on a search for stolen plutonium.
       All the clues lead them to a little Adriatic island.

864   Kauffman, Ray F. Coconut Wireless. New York:
       Macmillan, 1948.
           American mining engineer Bob Graydon is the
       hero of this spy novel set in Malaya during the
       closing days of the Japanese occupation.

865   Keeley, Edmund. The Imposter. Garden City, N.Y.:
       Doubleday, 1970.
           CIA agent Sam Kean leaves his love, goes to
       Greece where he is involved with Cypriot spies,
       reunites with his first girl after dallying with a
       second, and returns to America and an uncertain
       fate.

866   Keller, Beverly. The Baghdad Defections. Indian-
       apolis: Bobbs-Merrill, 1973.
           A German scientist has devised the ultimate in
       bio-chemical warfare and the Arabs, having cap-
       tured him, plan to use his knowledge to build a
       strong alliance of all the Arab countries against
       Israel.

867   Kelly, Judith. Diplomatic Incident. Boston: Houghton-
       Mifflin, 1949. Y
           When a Russian peace party mission arrives in
       Washington, an American State Department agent
       falls in love with one of their important delegates.
       When America rejects the Soviet offer, she is re-
       turned to Russia for "processing." An excellent

example of early Cold War intrigue stories in which
not a kind thought can be spared for the Russians.

868 Kelly, Michael. Assault. New York: Harcourt,
1967. *
Four men of British Special Operations are
parachuted into a field near Copenhagen with orders
to take out a nearby Nazi factory codenamed
"Knightsbridge."

869 Kennedy, Adam. The Domino Principle. New York:
Viking, 1975.
An unnamed intelligence agency employs an ex-
con as a political assassin in the U.S. Shades of
current headlines!

870 Kenyon, Michael. May You Die in Ireland. New
York: Morrow, 1965.
Willie Foley is off to claim an ancestral home
in the land of shamrocks, but unbeknownst to him,
his travel agency manages to sneak secret micro-
dots into his luggage.

871 Kenyon, Paul. The Ecstasy Connection. New York:
Pocket Books, 1974. P
The heroine of this author's writing is The
Baroness who appears to the outside world as
simply an international playgirl. Those in the
know (which now includes you) soon find that she
is a top adventureress-agent à la Modesty Blaise.
In this first of what appears to be a rather popular
series, she is involved in a monstrous plot replete
with sex and considerable violence. Others are:

872 _____. Death Is a Ruby Light. New York:
Pocket Books, 1974. P

873 _____. Diamonds Are for Dying. New York:
Pocket Books, 1974. P

874 _____. Flicker of Doom. New York: Pocket
Books, 1974. P

875 _____. Hard-Core Murder. New York: Pocket
Books, 1974. P

876 _____. Operation Doomsday. New York: Pocket
Books, 1974. P

877   Kessel, Joseph. <u>Army of Shadows</u>. Transl. from
       French by Haakon Chevalier. New York: Knopf,
       1944. *
       French Resistance battles the Nazis.

878   Kiefer, Warren. <u>The Lingala Code</u>. New York:
       Random House, 1972.
       Michael Vernon, the CIA's resident trouble-
       shooter in Leopoldville, the Congo, in the 1960s,
       was a busy man, but never more active than when
       he tried to solve the murder of his ex-Air Force
       buddy.

879   Kielland, Axel. <u>Dangerous Honeymoon</u>. Boston:
       Little, Brown, 1946. *
       A Swedish industrialist marries an American
       OSS agent to help her get the secrets of the V-2
       rocket out of Berlin.

880   Kirk, Lydia. <u>The Man on the Raffles Verandah</u>.
       Garden City, N.Y.: Doubleday, 1969.
       A rather poor ex-British agent has retired to
       Singapore where he has just enough capital to allow
       himself one gin each day on his hotel's verandah,
       but one day a letter arrives from his former
       chief....

881   Kirst, Hans H. <u>Hero in the Tower</u>. Transl. from
       the German by J. Maxwell Brownjohn. New York:
       Coward-McCann, 1972. *
       A crack German anti-aircraft unit is constantly
       besieged by a series of mysterious "accidents."

882   Knapp, Gregory C. <u>Stranglehold</u>. Boston: Little,
       Brown, 1973.
       A U.S. military intelligence agent is put on the
       trail of a young lieutenant who has disappeared from
       his Korean base. Soon the fellow is found in Japan,
       fought over by a couple of fanatical groups who want
       him for anti-American purposes.

883   Knebel, Fletcher. <u>Vanished</u>. Garden City, N.Y.:
       Doubleday, 1968.
       When a prominent Washington attorney disappears,
       the President forbids CIA involvement. It looks as
       though a juicy scandal may be brewing!

884   Knipscheer, James M. Code Three. By James M.
        Fox, pseud. Boston: Little, Brown, 1953.

885   _____. No Dark Crusade. By James M. Fox,
        pseud. Boston: Little, Brown, 1954.
        A tale of intrigue set against the backdrops of
        Paris, Rotterdam, Cologne, and New York.

        Knowlton, Winthrop, coauthor see Goodman,
        George J. W.

886   Koontz, Dean R. Hanging On. New York: Evans,
        1973. H*
        A company of GI misfits is air-dropped into
        France by a slightly crackpot general to carry out
        a demented secret mission. A clandestine M*A*S*H.

887   Kuhn, Edward, Jr. The American Princess. New
        York: Simon & Schuster, 1971.
        When an American girl marries the prince of a
        little Asian country on China's border, she finds
        her ex-boyfriend, a CIA agent, has come along too.

888   Kuniczak, W. S. The Sempinski Affair. Garden City,
        N. Y. : Doubleday, 1970.
        In Central Europe to examine some ancient
        documents relative to the trial and execution of
        Christ, O. H. Shippe uncovers a plot by a splinter
        group to assassinate the Soviet premier and put the
        blame on America.

889   Kyle, Duncan. A Cage of Ice. New York: St. Mar-
        tin's Press, 1971.
        Take one innocent-looking envelope postmarked
        Moscow that contains an unimportant paper on hydro-
        electricity and deliver it by mistake to a surgeon in
        New York. What do you have besides poor mail
        service? Naturally, a plot against the world.

890   _____. Flight into Fear. New York: St. Martin's
        Press, 1972.
        Shaw is a pilot and, on the side, an operative
        for British Intelligence. His current mission is to
        take a heavy package to San Francisco in the "regu-
        lar" manner and on his return, to smuggle a secret
        passenger into England.

891   _____. A Raft of Swords. New York: St. Martin's
           Press, 1974.
           A desperate race is undertaken to defuse six
           nuclear missiles on the ocean floor.

892   _____. The Suvarov Adventure. New York: St.
           Martin's Press, 1974.
           The Russians wish to obtain a long-immersed,
           but still lethal, missile from the depth near Van-
           couver Island. To do the work, they kidnap a
           British torpedo recovery expert.

893   _____. Terror's Cradle. New York: Viking,
           1975.
           A correspondent acting as an unwilling courier
           for both the KGB and the CIA, seeks to locate a
           tiny piece of microfilm which holds the fate of sev-
           eral governments.

894   Lambert, Derek. Angels in the Snow. New York:
           Coward-McCann, 1969.
           A young British diplomat on his first assign-
           ment in Moscow becomes involved with three people
           of various backgrounds: his beautiful Russian lan-
           guage teacher, an experienced, blasé, CIA agent,
           and a British defector who still has a dream of once
           more seeing his homeland.

895   _____. Kites of War. New York: Coward-
           McCann, 1969.

896   _____. The Red House. New York: Coward-
           McCann, 1972.
           A Soviet diplomat assigned to Washington during
           the 1968 Czech crisis must consider not only his
           daughter's disaffection but his own loyalty as well.

897   _____. The Yermakov Transfer. New York:
           Saturday Review Press, 1974.
           Russian computer expert heads a Zionist plot
           to kidnap Premier Yermakov and hold him hostage
           to get top Jewish physicists out of Russia and into
           Israel.

898   Landau, Mark A. For Thee the Best. New York:
           Duell, 1947.

899   _____. Nightmare and Dawn. By Mark Aldanov, pseud. Transl. by Joel Carmichael. New York: Duell, 1957.
While the American and Russian espionage establishments are concerned primarily with tricking one another, their operatives on the scene in Berlin, Venice, and Paris are more worried about their personal problems.

900   Landon, Christopher. Flag in the City. New York: Macmillan, 1954.
A bold hero, a sympathetic intelligence agent, a beautiful dame, and an elusive villain all cross paths in Iran during World War II.

901   Larauy, David. The Big Red Sun. New York: Prentice-Hall, 1971.
George Benachen, an amateur revolutionary, is sent by French Intelligence to Peking to arrange the defection of a high Communist official.

902   Lartéguy, Jean. The Bronze Drums. Transl. from French by Xan Fielding. New York: Knopf, 1968.
Francois Ricq is dropped into Laos in 1944 to form a resistance group for operations against the Japanese.

903   Lathen, Emma. Murder Against the Grain. New York: Macmillan, 1967.
When someone steals almost a million dollars from the Sloan Guaranty Trust, a Russian-American trade treaty is endangered. John P. Thatcher, hero of a number of other outright mysteries by this author, must get the money back and keep the deal on track.

904   Leasor, James. Passport for a Pilgrim. Garden City, N.Y.: Doubleday, 1969.
Dr. Jason Love, an admirer of judo and Cord motor cars, and agent McGillivray of MI6 seek missing persons in the Monastery of the Sacred Flame in Maloula. Other Love adventures are:

905   _____. Passport in Suspense. Garden City, N.Y.: Doubleday, 1967.

906   _____. Passport to Oblivion. Philadelphia: Lippincott, 1965.
Agent "K" disappears in Iran.

907   _____. Spylight. Philadelphia: Lippincott, 1966.
           First published in Britain as Passport to Peril.
           Dirty tricks in the Alps.

908   _____. Young Meridian. Philadelphia: Lippincott,
               1967.

909   le Carré, John. The Incongruous Spy: Two Novels
       of Suspense. 2 vols. in 1. New York: Walker,
       1964.
           Both of these titles will be examined here,
       rather than in separate entries. In Call for the
       Dead, agent George Smiley is concerned with the
       death of a British Foreign Office clerk who has
       just received security clearance. First published
       in Britain in 1961. A Murder of Quality again con-
       cerns operative Smiley, who must track down an
       East German Communist running amuck in an
       English public school building. Le Carré is prob-
       ably best known as the man responsible for entering
       the depressing, highly-realistic operative into the
       genre of secret agent literature. After le Carré,
       the cuteness, by and large, went out of the spy fic-
       tion (and movie) business and probably contributed
       in no small degree to its decline in vogue.

910   _____. The Looking Glass War. New York:
           Coward-McCann, 1965.
           A small espionage unit left over after World
       War II attempts to train one of its former agents
       for a mission into East Germany.

911   _____. A Small Town in Germany. New York:
           Coward-McCann, 1969.
           Agent Alan Turner arrives in Germany to find
       the crucial Green File and other secret papers
       stolen from the British embassy in Bonn.

912   _____. The Spy Who Came in from the Cold.
       New York: Coward-McCann, 1964.
           Alec Leamas, 50-year old professional British
       spy, has become a bit stale, but is offered one
       more assignment before his retirement. He lets
       himself be seduced into a pretended defection,
       thereby providing the East Germans with data from
       which they can establish that the head of their own
       espionage establishment is really a double agent.
       As much a landmark in the annals of spy fiction

as Fleming's Casino Royale (541).

913 _____. Tinker, Tailor, Soldier, Spy. New York:
Knopf, 1974.
Agent Smiley, himself suspect, much search
out and destroy the double agent in British Intelligence planted there years before by Moscow.

914 Lee, Elsie. The Spy at the Villa Miranda. New
York: Delacorte, 1967. Y*
Siri Quain accepts the companionship of a
sophisticated older woman visiting Greece. Soon
the lady reveals herself as more than just a fellow
tourist. This is one of those McInnes-type novels
of romance and violent suspense aimed at the female market.

Leonard, Charles L., pseud. see Heberden, Mary V.

915 Leslie, Peter. The Cornish Pixie Affair. (Girl from
U.N.C.L.E. Series, No. 3.) New York: Ace
Books, 1967. PH
The other two books on this lady agent, April
Dancer, were written by Michael Avallone and are
cited under his name above.

916 _____. The Gay Deceiver. New York: Stein &
Day, 1967.
A humerous British spy chase involving the
winner of a TV quiz program given a map to find
his 500-quid prize, and agents of MI6 engaged in a
plot to discredit an Arab leader and bring down the
price of Mideast crude.

917 _____, author see also Holly, J. Hunter

917 Lesser, Milton A. Come Over Red Rover. By
Stephen Marlowe, pseud. New York: Macmillan,
1968.
A double agent uses a U.S.I.A. official's kidnapped daughter to convince him to defect.

918 _____. The Search for Bruno Heidler. By Stephen
Marlowe, pseud. New York: Macmillan, 1966.
Ted Dunbar, working for the Army Graves Investigation Division, is asked to help find Nazi war
criminal Heidler.

919   _____. The Summit. By Stephen Marlowe, pseud.
        Cleveland: World, 1970.
             When Soviet troops mass on the Yugoslav bor-
        der and America prepares for action, a meeting
        between the President and the Premier is arranged
        for Geneva, complete with spies, kidnappings, and
        violence.   During the fictional James Bond era,
        this author also prepared a large number of parodies
        on the 007 theme.   These include:

920   _____. Danger Is My Line. By Stephen Marlowe,
        pseud. New York: Macmillan, 1960.   H

921   _____. Jeopardy Is My Job. By Stephen Marlowe,
        pseud. New York: Macmillan, 1961.   H

922   _____. Manhunt Is My Mission. By Stephen
        Marlowe, pseud. New York: Macmillan, 1963.   H

923   _____. Peril Is My Pay. By Stephen Marlowe,
        pseud. New York: Macmillan, 1960.   *

924   _____. Terror Is My Trade. By Stephen Mar-
        lowe, pseud. New York: Macmillan, 1958.   H

925   _____. Trouble Is My Name. By Stephen Mar-
        lowe, pseud. New York: Macmillan, 1956.   H

026   _____. Violence Is My Business. By Stephen
        Marlowe, pseud. New York: Macmillan, 1958.   H

927   Lestienne, Voldemar. Furioso. New York: St.
        Martin's Press, 1973.
             A French best seller, this yarn details the
        James Bondian adventures of four French Resis-
        tance commandos during World War II.   The quar-
        tet has all sorts of activities such that involve
        pretty girls, springing a stranger from the inner
        area of Dartmoor Prison, pretty girls, commandeer-
        ing the Prime Minister's car--along with its exalted
        occupant--pretty girls, taking on the SS inside Ger-
        many, and finishing up as it began, with les femmes.

928   Lewis, Norman. Flight from a Dark Equator. New
        York: Putnam, 1972.
             An American agent is sent to investigate a to-
        talitarian South American nation on the verge of
        revolution.

929   _____. The Sicilian Specialist. New York: Ran-
        dom House, 1975.

Mafia godfather Don Vincente dispatches hit-man
Marco Richards into the employ of the CIA, which in
turn sends him down to Texas on a very tough assignment.

930   . A Small War Made to Order. New York:
    Harcourt, 1966.
        An Englishman is hired to pose as a leftist re-
    porter, visit Cuba, and make the final reconnais-
    sance necessary for a proposed U.S. invasion.

931   Lilley, Tom. The Officer from Special Branch.
    Garden City, N.Y.: Doubleday, 1971.
        The Reds began a revolution in Malaya in 1948
    employing guerrilla troops much like the Viet Cong.
    Counterterrorist agents are part of a plan by the
    Projects Section of Great Britain to offset the Com-
    munist influence.

932   Linebarger, Paul M. A. Atomsk. New York: Duell,
    1949.
        An American army agent penetrates the Iron
    Curtain, purposefully leaves evidence of his visit,
    and returns to the United States to await develop-
    ments.

933   Lippincott, David. E Pluribus Bang. New York:
    Viking, 1971.
        One day in the future, the 39th U.S. President
    finds his bed compromised and shoots his wife.
    The CIA is called in to dispose of the evidence,
    but a few in the know commence blackmail proceed-
    ings. Soon, important bodies are lying all over
    Washington.

934   . The Voice of Armageddon. New York:
    Putnam, 1974.
        A criminal assassin has given the U.S. govern-
    ment pictures of himself, a timetable of planned
    killings, and 48 hours to stop him; a special group
    of agents is set up to deal with the problem. Then
    he changes the rules.

935   Littell, Blaine. The Dolorosa Deal. New York:
    Saturday Review Press, 1973.
        Samuel Webster, a Black operative for the
    highly secret U.S. "Projects Bureau," is ordered

to Israel to defuse a dangerous plot.

936   Littell, Robert.   The Defection of A. J. Lewinter.
Boston: Houghton-Mifflin, 1973. H
Lewinter is the inventor of a super garbage dis-
posal system and a defector to the U.S.S.R. While
he settles in to life in Moscow, agents of the KGB
are still trying to decide what they've got--while the
CIA wonders what, if anything, it may have lost.

937   Llewellyn, Richard.   But We Didn't Get the Fox.
Garden City, N.Y.: Doubleday, 1969.
In this sequel to no. 938, Edmund Trothe is off
on another high-level espionage adventure set off by
a bomb explosion, a kidnapping, and the theft of
some secret information.

938   _____.   The End of the Rug.   Garden City, N.Y.:
Doubleday, 1968.
Upon his return to England from an earlier
mission, Trothe is suckered back into his old secret agent role and hustled off to Germany to quash
a resurgent Nazi movement.

939   _____.   White Horse to Banbury Cross.   Garden
City, N.Y.: Doubleday, 1970.
Trothe discovers that two of his old colleagues
at "the shop" have penetrated his Anglo-Arabian oil
empire, knocked off some of his employees, and
are out to get him.   Two other Trothe stories are:

940   _____   Bride of Israel, My Love.   Garden City,
N.Y.: Doubleday, 1973.

941   _____.   Night Is a Child.   Garden City, N.Y.:
Doubleday, 1972.

942   Lockridge, Richard and George H. Estabrooks.   Death
in the Mind.   New York: Dutton, 1945.   *
An agent must discover who is committing a
series of treasonable acts inside the inner circles
of the British army and navy.

943   Lodwick, John.   Man Dormant.   New York: Duell,
1950.
First published in England under the title First
Steps Inside the Zoo.   A British spy works out of
the home of a wealthy eccentric American on the

French Riviera in the summer of 1949.

944 Loewengard, Heidi H. After Midnight. By Martha
Albrand, pseud. New York: Random House,
1948. Y*
An American veteran returns to Italy to relive
his wartime experiences and discover who betrayed
him to the Germans.
Readers may want to note that most of these
Albrand stories are a mixture of romance, mystery,
and espionage aimed primarily at ladies. The sex,
sadism, and mayhem of the Bond genre has been
toned down to a point where it is quite mild.

945 _____. A Call from Austria. By Martha Albrand,
pseud. New York: Random House, 1963. Y*
An American newsman comes to Vienna to find
his missing brother and finds a pretty girl who
bears him an old grudge.

946 _____. A Door Fell Shut. By Martha Albrand,
pseud. New York: New American Library,
1966. Y*
Circumstances trap a great violinist into ac-
cepting the job of secret agent.

947 _____. Hunted Woman. By Martha Albrand, pseud.
New York: Random House, 1952. Y*
A beautiful Czech woman attempting to flee to
Switzerland with her child is chased by Communist
agents and aided by a shy young American student.

948 _____. The Linden Affair. By Martha Albrand,
pseud. New York: Random House, 1957. Y*
A German, long a Russian prisoner, returns
to his wife and family and is given an important
post in the U.S. Security Department. A reporter
and a U.S. agent are suspicious.

949 _____. The Mask of Alexander. By Martha
Albrand, pseud. New York: Random House,
1955. Y*
The heroine is caught up with Italian Communists and neo-Nazis in postwar Venice and Paris.

950 _____. Meet Me Tonight. By Martha Albrand,
pseud. New York: Random House, 1960. Y*

In Brussels to meet her husband, the heroine
encounters instead one Farkas, reputedly responsible
for the imprisonment and deaths of many of her
friends and relatives in Hungary.   Soon it becomes
apparent that this is wrong. . . .

951   _____. Nightmare in Copenhagen.   By Martha
Albrand, pseud.   New York: Random House,
1954.   Y*
A Danish fisherman recovers secret explosives
from a wrecked German U-boat and is hounded by
Soviet agents;   then, a young American Scientist
mixes into the affair.

952   _____. No Surrender.   By Martha Albrand, pseud.
Boston: Little, Brown, 1942.   Y*
A young Dutch lawyer, secretly working for the
underground, accepts a government position under
the eye of the Gestapo and to the contempt of his
friends and neighbors.   First published serially in
The Saturday Evening Post.

953   _____. None Shall Know.   By Martha Albrand,
pseud.   Boston: Little, Brown, 1945.   Y*
Two young citizens of occupied France busy
themselves smuggling children into neutral Switzerland.   Captured by the Gestapo, the children of a
border town nearby contrive their freedom.

954   _____. Rhine Replica.   By Martha Albrand, pseud.
New York: Random House, 1969.   Y*
Up from Rome for the carnival in Cologne, the
hero finds the only room available to be in an old
castle out of town;   there he meets a beautiful girl
and is drawn into one of those sinister German
plots against world peace.

955   _____. Without Orders.   By Martha Albrand,
pseud.   Boston: Little, Brown, 1943.   Y*
An American soldier in undercover work with
the Italian underground movement.

956   Loraine, Philip. W.I.L. One to Curtis.   New York:
Random House, 1967.
The Western Intelligence Liaison, made up of
agents from Britain and America, attempts to fore-
stall the advent of a new leader in an unnamed

country by manipulating five of his intimates into influencing his withdrawal--permanently if necessary --from political life. Two others by this writer are:

957 _____. Break in the Circle. New York: Random House, 1951.

958 _____. Nightmare in Dublin. New York: Random House, 1964.

959 Lord, Graham. Marshmallow Pie. New York: Coward-McCann, 1970.
A British newspaperman is sent to see how the hippie movement functions. Undercover, he finds that its bearded leader has come up with a dangerous drug wanted by the agents of various unfriendly governments.

960 _____. The Spider and the Fly. New York: Viking, 1974. *
A spy romance involving a Member of Parliament and a "liberated" American divorcée.

961 Loring, Emilie (Baker). Love Came Laughing By. Boston: Little, Brown, 1950. *
A girl returns to Washington from South America carrying important secret papers and meets a Congressman with a dangerous political opponent.

962 Lorraine, John. Men of Career. New York: Crown, 1961.
Drastic changes in State Department functions and their unsettling effects on its personnel stationed in the intrigue-ridden Vienna of 1953 at the height of the Cold War and McCarthyism.

963 Lowden, Desmond. Bandersnatch. New York: Holt, 1969.
Retired Royal Navy Commander Alec Sheldon and his aging wartime crew plan to extract a cool £2 million from a Greek shipping mogul they've kidnapped.

964 Luard, Nicholas. The Robespierre Serial. New York: Harcourt, 1975.
Assigned to murder a defecting Arab leader, Carswell finds himself pursued across the Pyrenees

by local police and British/American agents.

965 _____. Warm and Golden War. New York: Harcourt, 1967.
Agents from "both sides" battle over a considerable sum in greenbacks.

966 Lucas, Ruth. Who Dare to Live. Boston: Houghton-
Mifflin, 1966. *
Englishwoman trapped in Germany by the out-
break of war in 1939, has her daughter taken by
the authorities. When the underground rescues her
child, she agrees to work with them in what becomes a seven-year struggle against terror.

967 Ludlum, Robert. The Matlock Paper. Cleveland:
World, 1973.

968 _____. The Osterman Weekend. Cleveland:
World, 1972.
A TV news executive is recruited by the CIA
to help break up a Soviet espionage ring codenamed
"Omega."

969 _____. The Rhineman Exchange. New York: Dial
Press, 1974.
An OSS agent travels to Buenos Aires in 1943
to meet a Gestapo agent and make an obscene trade
of diamonds for gyroscopes.

970 _____. The Scarlatti Inheritance. Cleveland:
World, 1971.
Nasty Ulster Scarlatti is using his money to
bankroll Hitler during World War II. A relative
who is also an American agent wonders where his
family's fortune is going.

971 Lyall, Gavin. Judas Country. New York: Viking,
1975.
An Eastern Mediterranean morass of espionage
and terrorists, Greco-Turkish tension, and the
sword of Richard the Lion-Hearted.

972 Lynn, Margaret. A Light in the Window. Garden
City, N.Y.: Doubleday, 1967.
In this cross between a romance and an es-
pionage tale (or, a spy romance), Rosanne seems

to be more disturbed about her husband's leaving
her for another than she is about his treason.

973   Lypsyte, Robert. Liberty Two. New York: Simon &
       Schuster, 1974.
            Former astronaut Charles Rice and his seem-
       ingly fantastic crusade to awaken the American peo-
       ple to sundry dangers is "helped" by an agent pro-
       vocateur in a semi-governmental group.

974   MacAlister, Ian. Strike Force 7. Greenwich, Conn.:
       Fawcett, 1974. P
            A band of mercenaries led by a cynical ex-army
       officer rescue two women from a terrorist strong-
       hold.

975   MacBeth, George. The Samurai. New York: Har-
       court, 1975.
            Girl agent battles Japanese nasties on Gibraltar.

       McCall, Anthony, pseud. see Kane, Henry

976   McCarry, Charles. The Miernik Dossier. New York:
       Saturday Review Press, 1973.
            A drunken Polish official on overseas duty is
       recalled. Fearing his reception, he elects to defect
       and various intelligence agencies, Western and
       Soviet, attempt to determine if his decision is true
       or if he is a double agent.

977   _____. The Tears of Autumn. New York: Satur-
       day Review Press, 1975.
            Agent Paul Christopher believes he knows who
       in the year of 1963 arranged for the killing of
       President Kennedy and why, but his theory is so de-
       structive he is ordered to stop, but he pursues it
       all the way, through Europe and Asia.

978   McCutchan, Philip. The Bright Red Businessmen.
       New York: John Day, 1969.
            Commander Shaw and the boys of MAX and D2
       must solve the mystery of the elastic water, a
       creeping natural disturbance that occurs in isolated
       areas.

979   _____. The Man from Moscow. New York: John
          Day, 1965.
          A group of Russian extremists, backed by the
          MVD, plans a coup in the Kremlin during a foreign
          ministers conference and simultaneously an "acci-
          dental" nuclear strike at Britain. Learning of this,
          British Intelligence dispatches Shaw.

980   _____. Moscow Coach. New York: John Day,
          1966.
          Shaw is sent on a bus trip to Moscow with or-
          ders to eliminate a fanatical British Communist who
          plans to assassinate the Russian leadership thereby
          allowing an extremist regime to take over and bring
          on an explosive war.   If you find this series en-
          joyable, here are other titles:

981   _____. All-Purpose Bodies. New York: John
          Day, 1970.

982   _____. Bluebolt One. New York: John Day, 1962.

983   _____. Dead Line. New York: John Day, 1966.

984   _____. Gibraltar Road. New York: John Day,
          1960.

985   _____. Hopkinson and the Devil of Hate. New
          York: John Day, 1961.

986   _____. On Course for Danger. New York: John
          Day, 1959.

987   _____. Poulter's Passage. New York: John Day,
          1967.

988   _____. Red Cap. New York: John Day, 1961.

989   _____. Screaming Dead Balloons. New York:
          John Day, 1968.

990   _____. Skyprobe. New York: John Day, 1968.

991   _____. Sladd's Evil. New York: John Day, 1965.

992   _____. Warmaster. New York: John Day, 1963.

          McDaniel, David, author see Holly, J. Hunter

993   McDonnel, Gordon. Crew of the "Anaconda." Boston:
          Little, Brown, 1940.   *
          A merchant becomes involved with espionage
          afloat.

994 _____. Intruder from the Sea. Boston: Little,
Brown, 1953. Y*
An American veteran vacationing in California
helps smash espionage ring. A good McCarthy era
piece.

995 McGeer, Patricia. Is There a Traitor in the House?
Garden City, N.Y.: Doubleday, 1965.
Section Q, American Intelligence, wants Selena
Mead to trace the connection between the near fatal
fall of a party girl and a Congressman seeking to
become Vice President.

996 _____. Legacy of Danger. New York: McKay,
1971.
Miss Mead is a Washington-based combination
of Modesty Blaise, Katy Touchfeather, and The
Baroness.

997 McGivern, William P. Caprifoil. New York: Dodd,
1972.
Title is the codename of a top French minister
who once operated in espionage with an American
and a British agent. Now he is missing and the
other two must find him. Other interesting stories
by this author include:

998 _____. Caper of the Golden Bulls. New York:
Dodd, 1966.
In Spain.

999 _____. Choice of Assassins. New York: Dodd,
1963.

1000 _____. Margin of Terror. New York: Dodd,
1954. *
Young American engineer in Rome drawn into
counterespionage.

1001 _____. Seven File. New York: Dodd, 1956.

1002 _____. Seven Lies South. New York: Dodd, 1960.

1003 McGovern, James. The Berlin Couriers. New York:
Abelard-Schuman, 1961. Y*
An aeronautical engineer is trained as a spy,
sent to East Berlin, captured, and put on public
trial. Sentenced to death, he is saved by the uprising of 1953.

1004   MacInnes, Helen (Mrs. Gilbert Highet). Above Suspi-
        cion. New York: Harcourt Brace, 1954. Y*
            First issued in 1941, this is the first in a long
        line of spy romances by this author. An Oxford
        don and his pretty wife are chosen to perform a
        secret mission to Germany in late 1939. While
        using their vacation as a cover, they are to find
        the whereabouts of an anti-Nazi agent. The plan
        was foolproof--until someone betrayed them!
            Readers of these MacInnes stories will find
        that they rank alongside those by Martha Albrand
        in their appeal. The action is suspenseful, but not
        as sadistic or bloody as that penned for male
        readers and the sex is much more tastefully handled.

1005   _____. Assignment in Brittany. Boston: Little,
        Brown, 1942. Y*
            A young British officer is sent to Occupied
        France in the guise of a wounded French soldier
        to learn what the Germans planned to do with the
        French coast. Almost too late, he discovers im-
        portant gaps in his information.

1006   _____. Decision at Delphi. New York: Harcourt,
        1960. Y*
            Strang and his Greek-American friend Kladas
        are to meet in Greece on a magazine assignment.
        Steve disappears, leaving some clues. His news-
        paper sends a resourceful young woman to take his
        place; soon she and Strang are involved in a web
        of intrigue stretching back to World War II.

1007   _____. The Double Image. New York: Harcourt,
        1966. Y*
            An American encounters a favorite former pro-
        fessor on a Paris street one day, which leads him
        to a Nazi-Soviet espionage caper and to the Greek
        island of Mykonos.

1008   _____. I and My True Love. New York: Har-
        court, 1953. Y*
            Against the backdrop of diplomatic intrigue and
        political maneuvering in Washington, two lovers are
        caught between Red spies and the American govern-
        ment's then-current fear of Communists in govern-
        ment. An excellent portrayal of the McCarthy era.

1009   _____. Message from Malaga. New York: Har-
           court, 1973. Y*
           Hopping about Spain from one espionage caper
           to another, it seems that Russian agents are always
           ahead of their American counterparts. Why?

1010   _____. Neither Five nor Three. New York: Har-
           court, 1951. Y*
           A publisher discovers his magazine is being
           subtly employed to disparage and undermine faith
           in America.

1011   _____. North from Rome. New York: Harcourt,
           1968. Y*
           A young American stumbles onto a vicious under-
           world syndicate and quickly finds himself caught up
           in a web of murder, espionage, and international
           intrigue.

1012   _____. Pray for a Brave Heart. New York: Har-
           court, 1955. Y*
           Two agents are embroiled in an effort to re-
           cover the Hertz diamonds, which a Communist ring
           has earmarked to fight democracy.

1013   _____. The Salzburg Connection. New York: Har-
           court, 1968. Y*
           A hardheaded Yankee did not know that his Aus-
           trian business trip would draw him into a suspense-
           ful chase for a chest hidden in an Alpine lake or
           that death and a beautiful woman waited in the sha-
           dows.

1014   _____. The Snare of the Hunter. New York:
           Harcourt, 1974. Y*
           Political intrigue revolves around Irinia Kusak's
           flight from Czechoslovakia in search of her Nobel
           Prize-winning father.

1015   _____. The Venetian Affair. New York: Harcourt,
           1963. Y*
           A raincoat switch suckers an American reporter
           on vacation in Paris into a Red plot to blame the
           anticipated assassination of DeGaulle on the United
           States. Although the subject matter is much the
           same, this tale is not the equal of Forsyth's The
           Day of the Jackal (566).

1016   MacKay, Lewis H. The Third Force. By Hugh
        Matheson, pseud. New York: Washburn, 1961.
            An English inventor produces a secret weapon
        and then becomes involved in the sundry plots of the
        big powers to grab it.

1017   McKelway, St. Clair. The Edinburgh Caper. New
        York: Holt, 1963.
            A New York crime fighter on vacation in Scot-
        land discovers a Red plot to kill Ike, Khrushchev,
        and Prince Philip when they arrive for a visit.
        Based on a shorter version first appearing in The
        New Yorker magazine.

1018   Mackenzie, Donald. Double Exposure. Boston:
        Houghton-Mifflin, 1963.
            A professional thief is released from prison in
        exchange for his agreement to visit Düsseldorf and
        pull off a delicate safe-rifling job for British Intelli-
        gence.

1019   _____. Salute from a Dead Man. Boston:
        Houghton-Mifflin, 1966.
            Released from a British jail, a Canadian goes
        straight until waitress Linda Swan passes him a
        roll of secret microfilm one day at lunch. Two
        similar yarns are:

1020   _____. Night Boat from Puerto Verde. Boston:
        Houghton-Mifflin, 1970.

1021   _____. The Quiet Killer. Boston: Houghton-
        Mifflin, 1968.

1022   MacKinnon, Allan. Assignment in Iraq. Garden City,
        N. Y.: Doubleday, 1961.
            A young Scottish tutor in Iraq and international
        intrigue. Others are:

1023   _____. Cormorant's Isle. Garden City, N. Y.:
        Doubleday, 1962.
            A kidnapping, Scottish scenery, Turkish politics,
        suspense.

1024   _____. House of Darkness. Garden City, N. Y.:
        Doubleday, 1947.

1025   _____. Map of Mistrust. Garden City, N. Y.:
        Doubleday, 1948.

1026 _____. Report from Argyll. Garden City, N. Y. :
Doubleday, 1964.
London reporter, Soviet agent, the Scottish
highlands.

1027 _____. Summons from Baghdad. Garden City,
N. Y. : Doubleday, 1958.

1028 McLartz, Nancy. Chain of Death. Garden City,
N. Y. : Doubleday, 1962.
An American girl on holiday in Guatemala is
tangled up with a U. S. Army officer in this tale of
treason, intrigue, murder, and romance.

1029 MacLean, Alistair. Bear Island. Garden City, N. Y. :
Doubleday, 1971. Y*
A Hollywood film crew sets up on location in
the Arctic, but soon it is revealed that one of its
members is a mass-murderer using the cover for
some nasty business while another is the British
agent sent to look into the affair.
Of all those who have written adventure-espion-
age stories, Mr. MacLean, by and large, is the one
whom readers can most rely upon for a maximum
of action and suspense and a minimum of unneces-
sary sex. His closest competitor, in this com-
piler's estimation, is Colin Forbes, whose works
are cited above. For well-written escapism, the
reader would need to read a great number of the
stories cited herein to find any that are consistently
better.

1030 _____. The Black Shrike. By Ian Stuart, pseud.
New York: Scribner's, 1962. Y*
British agent John Bentall is assigned to find
eight scientists and their wives who have disappeared en route to Australia. His search leads
him to an island in the far Pacific where a deadly
new super-missile, "The Black Shrike," is being
tested.

1031 _____. Caravan to Vaccares. Garden City, N. Y. :
Doubleday, 1970. Y*
Every year for centuries the gypsies have
gathered in a small French tourist town to honor
their patron saint. This time, however, the pil-
grimage is not so innocent; the caravan is a cover

for a sinister conspiracy. Only a few know the group's secret, the hiding of Russian rocket fuel experts; discovery may cost them their lives.

1032 _____. Circus. Garden City, N. Y. : Doubleday, 1975.
Three East German refugee trapeze artists ac-cept a CIA job: the removal of a deadly formula from behind the Iron Curtain.

1033 _____. The Dark Crusader. By Ian Stuart, pseud. New York: Scribner's, 1965. Y*

1034 _____. Fear Is the Key. Garden City, N. Y. : Doubleday, 1961. Y*
A British soldier being tried for illegal entry shoots his way out of a Florida courtroom, kidnaps a girl, and escapes. Never fear, it is our hero's cover for investigating a gang operating a mysterious salvage operation from an offshore oil rig in the Gulf of Mexico.

1035 _____. Force 10 from Navarone. Garden City, N. Y. : Doubleday, 1969. Y*
Three members of the team that destroyed the famous Guns (see 1037) are dropped into wartime Yugoslavia to rescue the leaders of previous mis-sions there and, incidentally, to destroy an im-portant enemy-held bridge in the mountains.

1036 _____. The Golden Rendezvous. Garden City, N. Y. : Doubleday, 1962. Y*
A tactical nuclear weapon and its creator are missing in the Caribbean and must be recovered at all cost.

1037 _____. The Guns of Navarone. Garden City, N. Y. : Doubleday, 1957.
In what has to be ranked as one of the best clandestine operation stories of all time, a small band of British commandos set out to destroy a pair of huge cannon covering a Grecian strait.

1038 _____. Ice Station Zebra. Garden City, N. Y. : Doubleday, 1964. Y*
When a capsule containing satellite reconnais-sance photos lands near the British Arctic

meteorological station Zebra, a worker locates it
and begins sending out signals. The American nuclear submarine Dolphin races to the site, carrying
aboard an undercover British intelligence officer
and a Russian defector. When after an almost fatal
crash dive, the "Allies" emerge near the station
and nearly succeed in recovering the capsule, a con-
tingent of Soviet paratroops drop in with the same
idea in mind.

1039 _____. Night Without End. Garden City, N. Y. :
Doubleday, 1960. Y*
     An airliner crashes near an Arctic IGY camp
and, several murders later, ...

1040 _____. The Peking Payoff. By Ian Stuart, pseud.
New York: Macmillan, 1975. Y*
     Hong Kong's leading businessman travels to
China for an audience with the Red premier and
becomes involved with Politburo fanatics who want
to assassinate their leader.

1041 _____. Puppet on a Chain. Garden City, N. Y. :
Doubleday, 1969. Y*
     An action adventure/intrigue/detective story
involving an Interpol agent sent to get the goods on
a nasty narcotics gang operating out of Holland.
The book opens and closes with scenes of a huge
crane overlooking an urban renewal project, thereby reflecting the title.

1042 _____. The Satan Bug. By Ian Stuart, pseud.
New York: Scribner's, 1962. Y*
     Someone has swiped a dangerous germ from the
Mordon Microbiological Research Establishment and
Pierre Cavell must find it before its new owners
can use it against the world.

1043 _____. Secret Ways. Garden City, N. Y. : Doubleday, 1959. Y*
     A cynical American adventurer is paid $60,000
by British Intelligence to induce an aging underground leader and professor to leave Budapest.
Posing as a newsman, he gets into Hungary easily
enough, but soon discovers that he may not even be
able to escape himself, let alone with his quarry in
tow.

1044   _____. The Way to Dusty Death. Garden City,
N.Y.: Doubleday, 1973. Y*
Johnny Harlow, "golden boy of the Grand Prix
circuits," is secretly working for the British in
their efforts to bag some ruthless heroin smugglers
who have penetrated the auto racing world.

1045   _____. When Eight Bells Toll. Garden City,
N.Y.: Doubleday, 1966. Y*
Philip Calvert of Britain's secret service is
called upon to stop a gang of modern-day pirates
operating in the islands off the west coast of Scotland.

1045   _____. Where Eagles Dare. Garden City, N.Y.:
Doubleday, 1968. Y*
Eight Allied agents, headed by Major John
Smith of MI6, are parachuted into the Bavarian
Alps to rescue an American general from an iso-
lated cliffside castle, the Schloss Adler. Shortly
after landing, one of these magnificent seven is
killed; Smith figures a traitor is in their midst.
They move to a village near the cliff, take on two
female agents, and prepare for their gamble.
While the two girls make it into the castle,
another teammate is murdered and all but Smith
and an American Ranger are taken. These two
then make their way to the castle via a cable car
and after several bad moments, complete their mission, returning to the village atop a cable car in a
very hairy fight. (Oh yes, en route home he who
was the traitor is identified.)

1046   McLean, Robinson. Baited Blond. New York: Mill,
1948. *
An American intelligence officer attempts to
locate three missing parts of a diagram for his
country's new strategic bombing mechanism.

1047   McLeave, Hugh. Only Gentlemen Can Play. New
York: Harcourt, 1974.
Based on a quote from Reinhard Gehlen, this
tale concerns an English spy who must perform a
mission for both his own service and the KGB
knowing that he will be a dead man if caught by
either.

1048 _____ . Steel Balloon. New York: Harcourt, 1964.

1049 _____ . Vodka on Ice. New York: Harcourt, 1969.
Enroute to a scientific conference in Sofia, Bob
McIllhenney is watched by Soviet agent Karen, who
loves to show off that native-Russian product, Vodka.

1050 MacLeod, Robert. Cave of Bats. New York: Holt,
1966.
U.N. "peacemaker" Cord, in Burma to settle
a labor dispute involving the building of a dam,
soon learns that China is attempting to halt the
facility's construction. Cord must find a way to
block them.

1051 _____ . The Iron Sanctuary. New York: Holt,
1967.
When Cord goes to Africa to look into the
mysterious plane crashes in Lake Calu, he is
plunged into a whirlpool of sabotage, smuggling,
and sudden death.

1052 _____ . Place of Mists. New York: McCall, 1970.
After an assassination in New York, Cord is
ordered to Morocco to protect a visiting dignitary
and the action takes him from there to the Atlas
Mountains, where a strange mist always rises in
the morning.

1053 Maggio, Joe. The Company Man. New York: Putnam, 1972.
A yarn of modern espionage which exposes the
shadow world of the CIA. Classified as fiction,
but based on the author's real-life adventures with
"the company" from the Bay of Pigs to Laos to the
Congo.

1054 Magowan, Ronald. Funeral for a Commissar. New
York: Roy, 1970.
MI5's most ruthless killer is ordered to un-
cover Russian penetration of the top echelons of
British industry.

1055 Mair, George B. The Day Khrushchev Panicked.
New York: Random, 1962.
Learning about "antimatter" at a 1958 embassy
party in Moscow, the hero launches an investigation

that involves agents from both sides of the Cold
War in a massive Soviet plot for world domination.

1056 _____. Death's Foot Forward. New York: Random House, 1964.
Dr. David Grant, N.A.T.O.'s head security
agent is sent to capture the Russian scientist who
developed "space sickness" and introduced it to the
West.

1057 _____. Miss Turquoise. New York: Random
House, 1965.
Grant must battle Chinese nasties and the
strange man called Zero to gain control of a rare
metal found only in the Spanish Sahara. Other
titles in the Dr. Grant series:

1058 _____. Black Champagne. New York: Random
House, 1968.

1059 _____. The Girl from Peking. New York: Random House, 1967.

1060 _____. Kisses from Satan. New York: Random
House, 1965.

1061 _____. Live, Love, and Cry. New York: Random House, 1966.

1062 Mallory, Drew. Target Manhattan. New York:
Putnam, 1975.
Piloting his vintage B-17 over New York, a
legendary aircraft designer, now on hard times,
demands a $5 million ransom or he will start
dropping 500-pound bombs.

1063 Manchester, William R. Beard the Lion. New York:
Mill, 1959.
An American pharmacologist involuntarily finds
himself bearing a document which proves a con-
spiracy between the Cypriotes and a faction of the
Nasser Government.

1064 Manning, Adelaide F. O. and Henry Coles. Alias
Uncle Hugo. By Manning Coles, pseud. Garden
City, N.Y.: Doubleday, 1952.
Secret agent Thomas Elphinstone Hambledon of
British Intelligence is Behind the Iron Curtain to
rescue a small boy who is the future king of a

little European mini-state.

1065 _____. All That Glitters. By Manning Coles,
pseud. Garden City, N.Y.: Doubleday, 1954.
Hambledon becomes involved in a high-powered
plot/counter-plot against world peace featuring the
MVD, the Bonn Security Police, assorted Berlin
crooks, and a couple of Polish fanatics.

1066 _____. Drink to Yesterday. By Manning Coles,
pseud. New York: Knopf, 1941.
Hambledon goes to Germany, impresses the
Nazis with his hatred of England, is recruited and
sent back to Britain as a spy. In short, he becomes a double agent, undergoing a process which
forever changes his pre-war life style and leads
to all the following works but the next.

1067 _____. Duty Free. By Manning Coles, pseud.
Garden City, N.Y.: Doubleday, 1959. H
A satirical story of intrigue in which a money-
pinch leads a little country to stage and quickly sup-
press a Communist revolution thereby bringing in an
American Economic Mission. Written on the order
of another great satire, The Mouse That Roared.

1068 _____. The Exploits of Tommy Hambledon. By
Manning Coles, pseud. Garden City, N.Y.:
Doubleday, 1959.
The adventures of our British agent comprised
in the reprinting of these three novels all entered
with annotation above and below: Alias Uncle Hugo,
Drink to Yesterday, and Toast to Tomorrow.
Others in the Tommy Hambledon series are:

1069 _____. Among Those Absent. By Manning Coles,
pseud. Garden City, N.Y.: Doubleday, 1948.

1070 _____. Basle Express. By Manning Coles, pseud.
Garden City, N.Y.: Doubleday, 1956.

1071 _____. Birdwatchers Quarry. By Manning Coles,
pseud. Garden City, N.Y.: Doubleday, 1956.

1072 _____. Brief Candles. By Manning Coles, pseud.
Garden City, N.Y.: Doubleday, 1954.

1073 _____. Come and Go. By Manning Coles, pseud.
Garden City, N.Y.: Doubleday, 1954.

1074 _____. The Concrete Crime. By Manning Coles,
pseud. Garden City, N. Y.: Doubleday, 1960.
Stolen secret data; France.

1075 _____. Dangerous by Nature. By Manning Coles,
pseud. Doubleday, 1950.
Soviets try to take over the Central American
republic of Esmeralda and destroy Panama Canal
with atomic missiles.

1076 _____. Death of an Ambassador. By Manning
Coles, pseud. Garden City, N. Y.: Doubleday,
1957.
Murder, jewels, art forgeries, political skull-
duggery on the continent.

1077 _____. Diamonds to Amsterdam. By Manning
Coles, pseud. Garden City, N. Y.: Doubleday,
1949.

1078 _____. The Far Traveler. By Manning Coles,
pseud. Garden City, N. Y.: Doubleday, 1956.

1079 _____. The Fifth Man. By Manning Coles, pseud.
Garden City, N. Y.: Doubleday, 1946.
Nazi sabotage ring in Britain

1080 _____. Green Hazard. By Manning Coles, pseud.
Garden City, N. Y.: Doubleday, 1945.
Smuggled into Nazi Germany under the alias of
a chemist, there to undermine the Reich.

1081 _____. Happy Returns. By Manning Coles, pseud.
Garden City, N. Y.: Doubleday, 1955.

1082 _____. House at Pluck's Gutter. By Manning
Coles, pseud. Garden City, N. Y.: Doubleday,
1953.

1083 _____. A Knife for the Juggler. By Manning
Coles, pseud. Garden City, N. Y.: Doubleday,
1965.
Russian is kidnapped and held in France.

1084 _____. Let the Tiger Die. By Manning Coles,
pseud. Garden City, N. Y.: Doubleday, 1947.

1085 _____. Man in the Green Hat. By Manning Coles,
pseud. Garden City, N. Y.: Doubleday, 1955.

1086 _____. Night Train to Paris. By Manning Coles,
pseud. Garden City, N. Y.: Doubleday, 1952.
Lost plans wanted by British and Russians.

1087 _____. No Entry. By Manning Coles, pseud.
Garden City, N. Y.: Doubleday, 1958.

1088 _____. Not Negotiable. By Manning Coles, pseud.
Garden City, N. Y.: Doubleday, 1949.
International counterfeiting ring.

1089 _____. Nothing to Declare. By Manning Coles,
pseud. Garden City, N. Y.: Doubleday, 1960.

1090 _____. Now or Never! By Manning Coles,
pseud. Garden City, N. Y.: Doubleday, 1951.
The missing son of Hitler and Eva Braun.

1091 _____. Search for a Sultan. By Manning Coles,
pseud. Garden City, N. Y.: Doubleday, 1961.

1092 _____. They Tell No Tales. By Manning Coles,
pseud. Garden City, N. Y.: Doubleday, 1942.
Hambleton solves wartime battleship explosions.

1093 _____. This Fortress. By Manning Coles, pseud.
Garden City, N. Y.: Doubleday, 1941.

1094 _____. Three Beams. By Manning Coles, pseud.
Garden City, N. Y.: Doubleday, 1957.

1095 _____. A Toast to Tomorrow. Garden City, N. Y.:
Doubleday, 1941.
Suffering from amnesia, a man enters the Nazi
party after years of aimless wandering; after the
Reichstag fire, he becomes Chief of the Nazi Police
--and also regains his memory.

1096 _____. With Intent to Deceive. By Manning Coles,
pseud. Garden City, N. Y.: Doubleday, 1947.

1097 _____. Without Lawful Authority. By Manning
Coles, pseud. Garden City, N. Y.: Doubleday,
1943.
An Englishman, unjustly discharged from the
Royal Tank Corps, enlists Hambledon to help un-
cover the Nazi spy who had him framed.

1098 Marchetti, Victor. The Rope-Dancer. New York:
Frosset & Dunlap, 1973.
The Deputy Director of the National Intelligence
Agency's special assistant is a double agent.

1099 Marin, A. C. The Clash of Distant Thunder. New
York: Harcourt, 1968.
CIA agent John Wells is ordered to Paris to

see why the resident spy has been missing his con-
tacts.

1100   _____. Rise with the Wind. New York: Harcourt,
          1969.
          A disillusioned American CIA agent of the
          LeCarré school is sent to a South American dicta-
          torship to spirit out a gibbering drunk believed to
          be a former top Nazi who skipped Germany at the
          close of the war with millions in Jewish gold.

1101   _____. A Storm of Spears. New York: Harcourt,
          1971.
          A disaffected teaching assistant is blackmailed
          into stealing a secret document from the research
          institute of a California university.

1102   Mariner, David. Countdown 1000. New York:
          Pinnacle Books, 1974. P
          Civilian pilot stumbles into a scheme to assas-
          sinate the participants in a summit conference.

1103   _____. Operation Scorpio. New York: Pinnacle
          Books, 1975. P
          MI5 must locate a secret Nazi bomb located
          somewhere in the Adriatic during the war.

          Markham, Robert, pseud. see Amis, Kingsley

1104   Markstein, George. The Cooler. Garden City, N.Y.:
          Doubleday, 1974.
          British agents, compromised and unhinged by
          their kill-training, are sent to the rest camp of
          Inverlock in Scotland, a jolly spot complete with all
          the amenities except location markers. Somehow
          a German agent gets within their midst and orders
          are passed up to find him. Strongly reminiscent
          of the Patrick McGoohan TV series "The Prisoner."

1105   Marlowe, Dan J. Operation Breakthrough. Greenwich,
          Conn.: Fawcett, 1972. P
          Earl Drake, "the man with nobody's face," and
          his beautiful girlfriend, Hazel, always seem to get
          the cases special agent Euhson's U.S. intelligence
          department cannot handle. Others in the series are:

1106   _____. Operation Checkmate. Greenwich, Conn.:
          Fawcett, 1973. P

1107 _____. Operation Deathmaker. Greenwich, Conn. :
      Fawcett, 1973. P

1108 _____. Operation Drumfire. Greenwich, Conn. :
      Fawcett, 1972. P
      A fantastic plot in San Francisco bankrolled by
      someone high in the Defense Department.

1109 _____. Operation Fireball. Greenwich, Conn. :
      Fawcett, 1972. P
      A mysterious genius owns his own fortified
      island.

1110 _____. Operation Flashpoint. Greenwich, Conn. :
      Fawcett, 1972. P

1111 _____. Operation Hammerlock. Greenwich, Conn. :
      Fawcett, 1974. P
      Brutal Mexican detective gets revenge on a
      corrupt politician.

1112 _____. Operation Stranglehold. Greenwich, Conn. :
      Fawcett, 1973. P

1113 _____. Operation Whiplash. Greenwich, Conn. :
      Fawcett, 1973. P
      A maverick Mafioso, Bolts Colisimo, has kid-
      napped Hazel.

1114 Marlowe, Derek. A Dandy in Aspic. New York:
      Putnam, 1966.
      Russian assassin Alexander Eberlin has devoted
      his life to cracking into the British Intelligence ap-
      paratus, where as a double agent he takes out var-
      ious of his Limey colleagues from time-to-time.
      One day, his English employers order him to seek
      out and destroy whoever is doing these terrible
      things; or, in other words, to assassinate himself!

1115 _____. Echoes of Celandine. New York: Putnam,
      1970.

1116 Marlowe, Hugh. Passage by Night. New York:
      Abelard-Schuman, 1964.
      Harry Manning, attempting to avenge the death
      of Maria Salas in the camp on the Isle of Tears,
      runs into an inferno of espionage more hideous than
      murder.

Marlowe, Stephen, pseud. see Lesser, Milton A.

1117   Marquand, John P. Stopover: Tokyo. Boston:
        Little, Brown, 1957.
            That wonderful Japanese superagent Mr. Moto
        appeared in a number of stories by this author
        during the 1930's. Unfortunately for the character,
        the real-life Japanese bombed Pearl Harbor in 1941
        and the wave of American indignation prevented his
        rehabilitation. This is the only post-war story to
        follow the detective-spy's activities and marks his
        final literary adventure. Two American intelligence
        agents are sent to break up a Communist espionage
        and terrorist ring operating in Tokyo and known to
        be planning anti-American riots.

1118   Marsh, James J. The Peking Switch. New York:
        McKay, 1972.
            An American spy plane pilot, captured and
        brainwashed by the Communist Chinese, is sent to
        the U.S. to destroy Russo-American disarmament
        talks.

1119   Marshall, Bruce. The Month of the Falling Leaves.
        Garden City, N.Y.: Doubleday, 1963.
            A British professor of philosophy lecturing in
        Warsaw is mistaken by the Reds for a secret agent.

1120   Marton, George and Tibor Meray. Catch Me a Spy.
        New York: Harper, 1970.
            On the first night of her honeymoon in Sofia,
        the police bust in and arrest Jessica Fenton's hus-
        band John. Shopping around, she learns that the
        only way to get him back is to catch a Russian spy
        and offer him in exchange.

1121   _____. The Three-Cornered Cover. New York:
        Harper, 1972.

1122   Mason, Colin. Hostage. New York: Walker, 1973.
            A shaky peace in the Mideast is shattered when
        a right-wing gang of Israelis steal some American
        strategic A-bombs stockpiled in Tel Aviv and use
        them to blow up Cairo. The Russians respond by
        sending a nuclear-missile submarine to Australian
        waters and holding the city of Sydney hostage until
        the U.S. and Britain give up their allegiance to
        Israel.

1123 Mason, Francis Van Wyck. <u>Dardanelles Derelict.</u>
Garden City, N. Y. : Doubleday, 1949.
Major Hugh North, top agent from Army G-2,
pretends to be a traitor, obtains an important Soviet
microfilm, and makes a hazardous mad dash from
behind the Iron Curtain to the "safety" of Turkey.

1124 _____. <u>The Deadly Orbit Mission.</u> Garden City,
N. Y. : Doubleday, 1968.
North, promoted to colonel, is sent to Tangier
to learn who has caused a Russian nuclear-warhead
missile to leave Soviet control and enter an orbit
over America.

1125 _____. <u>A Himalayan Assignment.</u> Garden City,
N. Y. : Doubleday, 1952.
Adventure and intrigue in Colonel North's
assignment to trap enemy agents up to no good in
Tibet.

1126 _____. <u>Maracaibo Mission.</u> Garden City, N. Y. :
Doubleday, 1966.
North is ordered to the shores of Lake Mara-
caibo with instructions to prevent sabotage to the
oil refineries there.

1127 _____. <u>Rio Casino Intrigue.</u> Garden City, N. Y. :
Doubleday, 1941.
North faces Nazi conspirators in Brazil.

1128 _____. <u>Saigon Singer.</u> Garden City, N. Y. :
Doubleday, 1946.
North searches for the Black Chrysanthemum,
key to the dossier of the imfamous Baron Tenno--
a list which contains the names of British and
American traitors in the wartime intelligence services.

1129 _____. <u>Secret Mission to Bangkok.</u> Garden City,
N. Y. : Doubleday, 1960.
North is ordered to prevent the kidnapping of a
famous American space scientist who is pursuing his
errant child through Thailand.

1130 _____. <u>Two Tickets for Tangier.</u> Garden City,
N. Y. : Doubleday, 1955.
North must reach Tangier to procure the

formula for thulium-X before it falls into the hands
of the nasties.

1131 _____. Zanzibar Intrigue. Garden City, N. Y.:
Doubleday, 1964.
A CIA agent has apparently defected to the
Soviet Union and Colonel North is charged with looking into the matter and "rescuing" the man if possible. Other Hugh North stories by this writer,
well known for his historical fiction, include:

1132 _____. The Gracious Lily Affair. Garden City,
N. Y.: Doubleday, 1957.

1133 _____. The Man from G-2. Garden City, N. Y.:
Doubleday, 1943.

1134 _____. Multi-Million Dollar Murders. Garden
City, N. Y.: Doubleday, 1960.

1135 _____. Trouble in Burma. Garden City, N. Y.:
Doubleday, 1962.

1136 Mason, Michael. 71 Hours. New York: Coward-
McCann, 1972.
Seventy-one hours before Soviet leaders are due
to arrive in America to conclude a disarmament
treaty, U. S. agents learn that someone is plotting
against the life of one of the negotiators. Whether
the Soviet premier or the American president they
do not know.

1137 Mason, Richard. The Fever Tree. Cleveland:
World, 1962.
English author and Communist agent is ordered
to assassinate the King of Nepal.

1138 Masters, John. The Breaking Strain. New York:
Dial Press, 1967.
A lady Russian scientist who plans defection to
America must overcome assorted difficulties, not
the least of which is the KGB and the U. S. intelli-
gence agency.

1139 _____. Thunder at Sunset. Garden City, N. Y.:
Doubleday, 1974.
The British are about to quit the mystical
mythical Southeast Asian country of Mingora, but
the new army commander and the Resident agent

  clash over a Communist terror group's attempt to take over the government.

1140 Masterson, Whit. The Man with Two Clocks. New York: Dodd, Mead, 1974.
  A California professor is conned into a spy caper which involves the use of his knowledge to fool Soviet reconnaissance satellites.

1141 Mather, Berkely. The Achilles Affair. New York: Scribner's, 1959.
  Peter Feltham's life is in danger because years ago he met and presently knows the identity of a top Middle East Communist agitator known only as Achilles.

1142 _____. The Pass Beyond Kashmir. New York: Scribner's, 1961.
  Idwal Rees, a Welshman, searches for secret papers which will reveal the location of huge oil deposits in the mountains of Kashmir.

1143 _____. Snowline. New York: Scribner's, 1973.
  Agent Rees works to crack the "Snowline," the trail of heroin moving via Bombay, the Seychelles, and North Africa to France. These Rees tales are about as much detective as spy, having considerable elements of both literary genre.

1144 _____. A Spy for a Spy. New York: Scribner's, 1968.
  Using a banking job as his Hong Kong cover, agent John Wainwright must arrange the exchange of a Russian held in England for a Britisher held in Communist China.

1145 _____. The Terminators. New York: Scribner's, 1972.
  British agent Rees is ordered to India, there to uncover evil doings and rescue friends in a country lousy with wily occidentals. Two others are:

1146 _____. The Break. New York: Scribner's, 1970.

1147 _____. Gold of Malabar. New York: Scribner's, 1960.

Matheson, Hugh, pseud. see MacKay, Lewis H.

1148   Maugham, Robert C. R.   Man with Two Shadows.   New
       York: Harper, 1959.
          A British agent finds himself handicapped by a
       personality dissociation resulting from injuries re-
       ceived during World War II.

1149   Maugham, William S.   Hour Before Dawn.   Garden
       City, N. Y.: Doubleday, 1942.
          The wife of a British general is suspected of
       being a German spy.

1150   Maxfield, Henry.   Legacy of a Spy.   New York:
       Harper, 1958.
          A leak in the American embassy at Zurich
       sends Slater to the Austrian Tyroll where he finds
       Communist and West German emissaries entangled
       with hotel-keeping, skiing, and the escape of an
       important Hungarian.

1151   Meiring, Desmond.   The Brinkman.   Boston: Houghton-
       Mifflin, 1965.
          The "brinkman," pursues his officially secret
       life of murder and intimidation in Laos and Vietnam
       only to be opposed by a sophisticated French news-
       man.

1152   Meissner, Hans.   Duel in the Snow.   Transl. from
       German by Erica Pomerans.   New York: Morrow,
       1942. *
          After the Japanese invasion of the Aleutians in
       1942, the Imperial High Command sends a group
       of Japanese meteorologists and scouts to the Alaskan
       Range to radio weather reports. Learning of this,
       the Americans send in their own team of scouts to
       capture or eliminate the "Nips."

1153   Melchior, Ib.   Order of Battle.   New York: Harper,
       1972.
          The discovery and destruction of the Nazis'
       fabled Werewolf Corps before the completion of its
       only mission--the assassination of General Eisen-
       hower.

1154   _____.   Sleeper Agent.   New York: Harper, 1975.
          Death duel between a Nazi "sleeper agent" due

to be planted in America and an American counter-
intelligence agent of German extraction.

1155   Merle, Robert. <u>The Day of the Dolphin.</u> Transl.
       from French by Helen Weaver. New York: Simon
       & Schuster, 1969.
            First published in France in 1967, this is the
       story of Professor Henry Sevilla and his two dol-
       phins, which he has trained to communicate with
       humans. These sea-going mammals are in turn
       believed of great value by the CIA for one of their
       schemes.

1156   Merrick, Gordon. <u>Hot Season.</u> New York: Morrow,
       1958.
            David Spofford is an intelligence agent assigned
       to one of America's unnamed Mediterranean em-
       bassies. During one five-day period, he attempts
       to get the Peoples' Choice elected in the host
       country's first, but rigged, election.

1157   _____. <u>The Strumpet Wind.</u> New York: Morrow,
       1947.
            An American intelligence officer helps the
       French Resistance.

1158   Merrick, William. <u>No One of that Name.</u> New York:
       Holt, 1965.
            An American minister is in an African nation
       where civil war threatens. There he finds an ap-
       parent Communist plot to take over the place, but
       when he attempts to get a mystical leader to step
       in and quash it, he is opposed by the cynical chief
       of the local CIA detachment.

1159   _____. <u>The Packard Case.</u> New York: Random
       House, 1961.
            Set in Paris, this is the story of agent
       Bradock's attempt to prevent Packard's defection
       to the Russians. In the process, we are treated
       to many flashbacks as Bradock reviews his career
       and his links to the escape-minded Packard.

1160   Mikes, George. <u>The Spy that Died of Boredom.</u> New
       York: Harper, 1974.
            The KGB is slipping up by flooding the West
       with a horde of half-trained agents. One of these,

whose story we follow, is sent to England to woo
secrets from susceptible young secretaries working
in defense agencies.

1161   Miller, Beulah M.   The Fires of Heaven.   Los
       Angeles: Douglas-West, 1974.
       Only three people knew the Arabian mission
       Weber was to undertake for the American govern-
       ment and only one man could prepare him for that
       assignment in time!

1162   Miller, Merle.   Secret Understanding.   New York:
       Viking, 1956.
       Matthews, a former OSS agent now a successful
       writer, is asked by his publisher (and indirectly by
       "J," the head of American counter-intelligence) to
       find out why a highly-decorated USAF ace would
       broadcast propaganda for Korea and then disappear.

1163   Mills, Osmington.   Traitor Betrayed.   New York:
       Roy, 1966.
       A superintendent at Scotland Yard who also
       works for that agency's Special Branch (in fact a
       super-secret spy organization) is sent to a scientific
       meeting disguised as a historian with orders to pre-
       vent one Mervyn Marshland's defection to the Soviets
       with a hat full of vital documents.

1164   Milton, Joseph.   The Death Makers.   New York:
       Lancer Books, 1966.   P
       One renegade American could ensure a Commu-
       nist victory in Vietnam unless secret agent Bart
       Gould could stop him.   Other titles in this exclusively
       paperback Bart Gould Espionage Series include:

1165   _____.   Assignment: Assassination.   New York:
       Lancer Books, 1964.   P

1166   _____.   Baron Sinister.   New York: Lancer Books,
       1965.   P

1167   _____.   Big Blue Death.   New York: Lancer Books,
       1965.   P

1168   _____.   The Man Who Bombed the World.   New
       York: Lancer Books, 1966.   P

1169   _____.   President's Agent.   New York: Lancer
       Books, 1967.   P

1170 _____. Worldbreaker. New York: Lancer Books,
        1964. P

1171 Minick, Michael. The Kung Fu Avengers. New York:
        Bantam Books, 1975.
        A brother-sister team of martial arts experts
        smash an international band of nasties.

1172 Mitchell, James. Death and Bright Water. New
        York: Morrow, 1974.
        Agent Callan must run interference from Rus-
        sian and British Intelligence to rescue a young
        woman under house arrest in Crete.

1173 _____. A Red File for Callan. New York: Simon
        & Schuster, 1971.
        After 16 exciting years with MI6 Callan began
        having such horrible nightmares that he had to re-
        tire. Then after six months at a dreary accountant's
        job, he decides he is recovered enough to come
        back for one last assignment.

1174 _____. Russian Roulette. New York: Morrow,
        1973.
        One day Callan received word that he is being
        deliberately sacrificed to the Russians for the ex-
        change of a more important agent.

1175 _____. Way Back. New York: Morrow, 1960.
        Henry Walker, a British foundry worker, re-
        lives his part in a Red bomb plot, and finds to his
        dismay that this knowledge is held by others who
        want him to pick up where he left off years before.

Monig, Christopher, pseud. see Crossen, Kendell F.

1176 Monsarrat, Nicholas. Smith and Jones. New York:
        Sloane, 1963.
        A pair of British diplomats defect to the "other
        side." A security officer known as "The Drill Pig,"
        who has charge of their files and is blamed for
        their walk-out, is sent to keep them under surveil-
        lance.

1177 Montross, David. Traitor's Wife. Garden City, N.Y.:
        Doubleday, 1962.
        Della Borden, a Berkeley California housewife,

meets a Communist agent who helps her join her
defecting scientist-husband in Moscow.   Two others
are:

1178 _____. Fellow-Travelers. Garden City, N. Y.:
Doubleday, 1965.

1179 _____. Troika. Garden City, N. Y.: Doubleday,
1963.

1180 Moorcock, Michael. The Chinese Agent. New York:
Macmillan, 1970. H
British agent Jerry Cornell is assigned to find
Kung Fu Tzu, the Local Red Chinese spy-in-resi-
dence (whose people had stolen and mislaid vital
secret plans).

1181 Moore, Robin. The Country Team. New York:
Crown, 1967.
The situation in a mythical Asian country (Vietnam?) deteriorates so badly that the local CIA team
must enlist the services of an American adventurer
who owns a rubber plantation in the nation.

1182 _____. Court Martial. Garden City, N. Y.:
Doubleday, 1971.
A Vietnamese counterspy is alleged to have been
murdered and a vindictive general orders five Green
Berets to stand trial for the "crime."

1183 _____. The Green Berets. New York: Crown,
1965.
The controversial story of U.S. Special Forces
in Vietnam that John Wayne made into a hawkish
movie; several sections deal with espionage and
clandestine operations.

1184 _____ and Al Dempsey. The London Switch. New
York: Pinnacle, 1974. P
Devoted to the world of electronic surveilliance
and pushbutton destruction, this yarn concerns a
man framed for murder and on the run. As much
a detective story as a spy thriller, incorporating
elements of both.

1185 Morgan, Brian S. Business at Blanche Capel. Boston: Little, Brown, 1954.
At a virus research station in Essex, the good

doctor and his beautiful assistant are working on an
agent (germ) of bacterial warfare. When the flask
containing the virus is taken, the two scientists set
out to pursue the thief across Europe. Not as good
as MacLean's The Satan Bug.

1186   Morris, John.   Fever Grass.   New York: Putnam,
        1969.
            Peter Blackmore, a wealthy Jamaican and
        marijuana user, is lured into a sort of unofficial
        local CIA complete with its own native targets.

1187   Morrow, Susan.   A Season of Evil.   Garden City,
        N.Y.:   Doubleday, 1970.   Y*
            Midge is in St. Croix because Quinn of the
        CIA is worried about a potential Black Power
        struggle on the little island.

1188   Moyes, Patricia.   Death and the Dutch Uncle.   New
        York: Holt, 1969.
            In this combination mystery/spy tale, Inspector
        Tibbett of Scotland Yard searches from England to
        the Netherlands for the answer to the question:
        "How does the killing of a small-time British pub
        owner affect an international dispute between two
        new African nations?"

1189   Mullally, Frederick.   The Assassins.   New York:
        Walker, 1966.
            Washington Post reporter in London falls in
        love with a Russian correspondent. Both are in
        town for the end of the Cold War, due to be brought
        about by the formal reunification of Germany. It
        turns out, however, that she is the niece of the
        Soviet premier and a member of a far-right Russian
        splinter group that plans to break up the festivities
        by killing her uncle.

1190   Munro, James.   Die Rich, Die Happy.   New York:
        Knopf, 1966.
            James Craig, top dog in Britain's hush-hush
        "K" department is assigned to protect a shipping
        tycoon about to fall into the hands of the Red
        Chinese. Published first in installments in Cos-
        mopolitan.

1191   _____.   The Innocent Bystanders.   New York:

Knopf, 1970.
The boss sends Craig on a desperate mission, from which he is not expected to return, with orders to find a scientist of immense importance.

1192 _____. The Man Who Sold Death. New York: Knopf, 1965.
Black Belt expert Craig did not plan on becoming a professional killer, but in this first of a series, Department "K" of MI6 recruited him as their one hope for the liquidation of St. Briac, the head of a radical group planning to draw England into the Algerian mess.

1193 _____. The Money that Money Can't Buy. New York: Knopf, 1968.
Craig and the KGB are in complete agreement in their search for the murderer of a Chinese waiter in a Lake District restaurant who was found with a phony $20 bill in his pocket.

1194 Murphy, John. Pay on the Way Out. New York: Scribner's, 1975.
A CIA trainee is plunged into the world of double-agents in Spain and Washington.

Murphy, Warren, coauthor see Sapir, Richard

1195 Nabarro, Derrick. Rod of Anger. New York: Sloane, 1954. *
Five years after the war, Englishman John Granger returns to Europe to pick up Anna, his love left behind in the underground. Another old friend, Anton, is now a fugitive from the party controlling Anna's nation and Granger attempts to help him escape from secret police chief Brud. In the finale, only two of the three escape, with the mean Brud claiming forfeit the life of the third.

1196 Nathanson, E. M. The Dirty Dozen. New York: Random House, 1965.
"Project Amnesty" called for the training of a dozen condemned criminals as super-secret commandos and the dropping of same behind enemy lines in France to take out a German headquarters just before D-Day.

1197 Nicole, Christopher. <u>The Captivator</u>. By Andrew
York, pseud. Garden City, N. Y. : Doubleday,
1974.
Jonas Wilde, code-named "The Eliminator" in
a special branch of British Intelligence, sets off in
his catamaran to deliver the ransom for a kidnapped
Western European princess. At sea he meets both
the kidnappers and a mighty storm.

1198 _____. <u>The Co-ordinator</u>. By Andrew York,
pseud. Philadelphia: Lippincott, 1967.
In this sequel to <u>The Eliminator</u> cited below,
agent Wilde is assigned to take out a man known to
the British as "The Swedish Falcon"--a fellow about
to betray Great Britain.

1199 _____. <u>The Deviator</u>. By Andrew York, pseud.
Philadelphia: Lippincott, 1970.
Agent Wilde has been unmasked by the KGB
and his upcoming mission to Russia may be fatal.

1200 _____. <u>The Eliminator</u>. By Andrew York, pseud.
Philadelphia: Lippincott, 1967.
In this first of the series, one of Wilde's su-
periors has defected to Russia and so "the Elimi-
nator" is sent forth to kill a sufficient number of
Soviet nasties until he can take out the turncoat.

1201 _____. <u>The Expurgator</u>. By Andrew York, pseud.
Garden City, N. Y. : Doubleday, 1973.
Someone is knocking off important Americans
visiting Britain. Agent Wilde's chief learns the
killer is named O'Dowd and lives in the village of
Dort in the Medoc region of France. Wilde is sent
over with orders to eliminate--and runs into a whole
clan of O'Dowds.

1202 _____. <u>The Fascinator</u>. By Andrew York, pseud.
Garden City, N. Y. : Doubleday, 1975.
Wilde must discover the would-be assassins of
an Arab prince whose relationship with the West is
vital to world peace.

1203 _____. <u>The Infiltrator</u>. By Andrew York, pseud.
Garden City, N. Y. : Doubleday, 1971.
Wilde infiltrates a gang causing all sorts of
mischief about the British Isles.

1204 _____. The Predator. By Andrew York, pseud.
Philadelphia: Lippincott, 1968.
Wilde is fired when his Five Star Photographic
Agency (an "Eliminator" section cover) is raided
and three of its people killed. Jonas wants to
avenge this setback, but his only lead is the disappearance in Rome of a CIA man who knew the
agency's address.
By and large, readers will find this series com-
parable to the legendary Bond tales.

1205 Noel, Sterling. Few Die Well. New York: Farrar,
1953.
A "hard-hitting-hard-kissing" tale of international intrigue in the post-war atomic age.

1206 _____. I Killed Stalin. New York: Farrar, 1951.
A yarn of intrigue and suspense concerning a
daring episode in the war of the near future. As
the Soviet dictator of our title died in 1953, readers
may have to substitute a different name.

1207 _____. Storm over Paris. New York: Farrar,
1956.
A ship's officer is drafted to impersonate an
international crook and turns immediately into a
violent man who succeeds in outwitting the intelligence heads of four nations.

1208 _____. Run for Your Life. New York: Farrar,
1958.

1209 Nolan, Frederick. The Algonquin Project. New
York: Morrow, 1974.
Our title refers to an OSS plot, apparently
approved by Eisenhower, to kill a loud-mouthed
Army Air Forces general (modeled on Patton) with
a hit-man supplied by Lucky Luciano.

1210 _____. The Retter Double-Cross. New York:
Morrow, 1975.
The British Ministry of Defense in 1940 puts
together a do-or-die MacLean-style band to drop
behind German lines to blow up a German nerve-
gas factory. Unfortunately for them, Retter, the
top Nazi agent in England, gets wind of the plan
and sets the Gestapo up for the catch.

1211 North, Anthony. Strike Deep. New York: Dial Press, 1974.
The codes to Pentagon computers containing ultra-classified data are in the hands of persons- or-person unknown but bent on America's destruction.

1212 Null, Gary. Cuban Expedition. New York: Pyramid Books, 1974. P
An international underground organization known as "The Secret Circle" works to right a monstrous plot involving American security and Castro's Cuba.

1213 O'Brien, Robert C. A. Report from Group 17. New York: Atheneum, 1972.
American agents discover a plot to poison the drinking water of Washington, D. C.

1214 O'Brine, Padraic Manning. No Earth for Foxes. New York: Delacorte, 1975.
Two tough-minded British operatives are sent to cooperate with Russian and American agents in finding and destroying an ex-Gestapo agent wanted for war crimes.

1215 _____. Mills. New York: Delacorte, 1969.

1216 _____. Passport to Treason. New York: Delacorte, 1955.

1217 O'Donnell, Peter. I, Lucifer. Garden City, N. Y.: Doubleday, 1967.
This, the third of the Modesty Blaise series, involves a young man named Lucifer, who can predict with 80% accuracy who is to die within a six month period. Modesty and her faithful friend Willie Garvin are asked to look into the matter.
Author O'Donnell began this female superagent's adventures as a 1962 cartoon strip for the London Evening Standard. She and Garvin were expressly designed as "high-camp" counterparts to James Bond (read in that spirit, these stories are not half bad); their motion picture exploits, while exceedingly amusing, were less than a boxoffice smash.

1218   _____. The Impossible Virgin. Garden City, N.Y.:
          Doubleday, 1971.
              Dr. Brunel and his friend Lisa draw Modesty
          and Willie to the site of their East German gold-
          mine, there to do them in. Even after such sundry
          trials as imprisonment in a cage with a belligerent
          gorilla, attacks by savages, and a death-struggle
          with the villains, they must somehow manage to es-
          cape the wasp-filled jungles of Ruanda. The fourth
          in the Blaise series.

1219   _____. Modesty Blaise. Garden City, N.Y.:
          Doubleday, 1965.
              The first of a five-volume series devoted to
          the gorgeous ex-mobstress and her faithful knife-
          toting companion, Willie Garvin. Having received
          all the benefits of a successful career in big-time
          crime, Modesty had "retired." Fit as a fiddle, but
          bored, she turns a willing hand when British Intelli-
          gence asks her to help with a Mideast crisis created
          by arch-villain Gabriel. In addition, Gabriel has
          snitched about £10 million worth of diamonds which
          need to be returned to their rightful owners. Call-
          ing up Garvin, now a successful pub owner, the
          two set out for the Mediterranean, where they are
          captured by Gabriel.

1220   _____. Sabre Tooth. Garden City, N.Y.: Double-
          day, 1966.
              Deep in a secret valley of the Hindu Kush, a
          lethal army of international desperadoes from a
          dozen countries is training in a diabolical plot to
          capture the oil-rich country of Kuwait. Modesty
          and Willie are asked to break up these terrible pro-
          ceedings.

1221   _____. A Taste for Death. Garden City, N.Y.:
          Doubleday, 1969.
              Modesty and Willie set out to rescue an archae-
          ological expedition from an arch-fiend and end up
          "sailing" across the Algerian desert in a desperate
          race against a cruel death.

1222   Offutt, Andrew. Operation Super Ms. New York:
          Warner Paperback Library, 1974. P
              Superspy Eve Smith is sent to check into a
          drug-smuggling caper in France. Sort of a cross

between Modesty Blaise and The Baroness.

1223   O'Hara, Kenneth. Sleeping Dogs Lying. New York:
        Macmillan, 1962.
        Checking up on the record of a scientist's girl-
        friend, an agent uncovers a four-year-old murder,
        security problems, and espionage.

1224   _____. Underhandover. New York: Macmillan,
        1963.
        Agent Bron Armine, technical advisor to a
        Central European state, is caught in a web among
        its three policing forces. Others are:

1225   _____. Double Cross Purposes. New York:
        Macmillan, 1962.

1226   _____. View to Death. New York: Macmillan,
        1958.

1227   Olson, Selma. Ana Mistral. North Hollywood,
        Calif.: Domina Books, 1975.
        A liberated woman agent in the mold of The
        Baroness.

1228   O'Malley, Mary D. The Dangerous Islands. By Ann
        Bridge, pseud. New York: McGraw-Hill, 1964. *
        Julia Probyn joins forces with Colonel Philip
        Jamieson of British Intelligence to locate Russian
        satellite tracking stations in the Hebrides.

1229   _____. Emergency in the Pyrenees. By Ann
        Bridge, pseud. New York: McGraw-Hill, 1965. *
        Julia has now married Col. Jamieson and when
        he is sent off to the Middle East, she elects to stay
        behind at his boyhood home in the Pyrenees to have
        their child. The baby is born prematurely and
        Julia is involved in a sabotage plot with international
        complications before hubby can return.

1230   _____. The Episode at Toledo. By Ann Bridge,
        pseud. New York: McGraw-Hill, 1966. *
        Julia sets out this story while her friend Hetta,
        wife of a British diplomat in Spain, has her hands
        full with two cases of Communist conspiracy aimed
        against VIP's from America.

1231   _____. The Lighthearted Quest. By Ann Bridge,

Macmillan, 1956. *
Julia Probyn goes off to the deserts of North
Africa to find a missing cousin and becomes in-
volved with the Moroccan freedom movement and the
Communist effort to take it over.

1232   _____. The Malady in Madeira. By Ann Bridge,
pseud. New York: McGraw-Hill, 1970. *
Recently widowed Julia Probyn visiting the lush
island of Madeira finds a clue to her husband's disappearance somewhere in Central Asia while on a
top-level mission. Armed with this information,
she takes over his job and discovers that the Russians are experimenting with nerve gas nearby.

1233   _____. Numbered Account. By Ann Bridge, pseud.
New York: McGraw-Hill, 1960. *
Julia becomes involved with the Soviet theft of
blueprints for nuclear submarine tankers from the
numbered Swiss account of her cousin Colin of
British Intelligence.

1234   _____. The Portugese Escape. By Ann Bridge,
pseud. New York: Macmillan, 1958. *
Julia arrives in Portugal to cover a wedding
and becomes involved in the escape of a Hungarian
priest, his Red pursuers, and a Hungarian countess
recently released from prison behind the Iron Curtain.

1235   O'Malley, Patrick. The Affair of Chief Strongheart.
New York: Morrow, 1964. H
A Harrigan and Hoeffler adventure.

1236   _____. The Affair of John Donne. New York:
Morrow, 1964. H
Agents Harrigan and Hoeffler are assigned to
infiltrate an ultra-far-right organization and prove
that it is really linked to the Communists.

1237   _____. The Affair of Jolie Madame. New York:
Morrow, 1964. H
Only a beautiful blond knows the fate of a missing computer scientist; Harrigan and Hoeffler must
convince her to reveal it.

1238   _____. The Affair of Swan Lake. New York:

Mill, 1962. H
   Counter-intelligence agents move into the lakes
area of Minnesota to smell out suspected hostile
anti-missile activities.

1239   _____. The Affair of the Blue Pig. New York:
   Morrow, 1965. H
      Agents Harrigan and Hoeffler stop off to help a
   detective friend solve a murder. This adventure
   verges more on being a mystery story than a spy
   yarn.

1240   _____. The Affair of the Bumbling Briton. New
   York: Morrow, 1965. H
      When England's foremost counter-espionage
   agent (Bond?) comes to America and promptly disappears, Harrigan and Hoeffler move to save him
   from a femme fatale holding him captive in northern
   California.

1241   _____. The Affair of the Red Mosaic. New York:
   Morrow, 1961. H
      In which the author introduces those two zany
   U.S. counter-intelligence agents, Harrigan and
   Hoeffler--the Abbott and Costello of espionage.

1242   O'Neill, Edward A. The Rotterdam Delivery. New
   York: Coward, 1975.
      Five nasties hijack a huge supertanker and holt
   it for a $25 million ransom.

Oram, John, author see Holly, J. Hunter

1243   Ordway, Peter. Face in the Shadows. New York:
   Wyn, 1953. *
      A newsman pegged as a Communist trails a
   Red agent all around the country and into Canada
   until he can capture him and prove himself a good
   security risk after all.

1244   Orvis, Kenneth. Night Without Darkness. New
   York: Coward-McCann, 1966.
      American agent Adam Beck must either kill or
   free Dr. Beldon, inventor of a paralysis mist more
   deadly than an H-bomb.

1245   O'Toole, George. An Agent on the Other Side. New

York: McKay, 1973.
Messages by a medium, conveying the reports
of double-agent Oleg Penkovsky (a real-life person)
warning of the 1968 invasion of Czechoslovakia, are
what our hero, John Sorel, maker of documentary
films and unwilling dupe of the CIA, finds himself
up against.

1246   Pace, Eric. Any War Will Do. New York: Random
       House, 1972.
       "The Firm" was a very private, all-powerful
       arms trading organization run with ruthless effi-
       ciency with profits from the Paris demi-mondc, the
       Sicilian underworld, and a labyrinth of Arab politics
       and African violence. Agent Harker was ordered in
       to break it up and put an end to its motto (the
       title).

1247   _____. Saberlegs. Clcveland: World, 1970.
       A German chemist who developed a poison gas
       during World War II plans to sell it to an Egyptian
       commando outfit unless a Jewish Nazi-hunting group
       can find "Saberlegs" first.

1248   Parker, Maude. The Intrigucr. New York: Rine-
       hart, 1952.

1249   _____. Invisible Red. New York: Rinehart, 1953.
       After a seven-year stay in Russia, a young
       American girl returns to America only to be met
       at the airport with a warrant for her arrest as a
       Communist spy. A lawyer who loved her years be-
       fore risks his career to prove her innocent.

1250   Parker, Robert B. Passport to Peril. New York:
       Rinehart, 1951.

1251   _____. Ticket to Oblivion. New York: Rinehart,
       1950.
       With the help of a beautiful redheaded counter-
       spy and a group of Maquis, an American agent in
       France succeeds in preventing the Russians from
       hijacking a shipment of French gold.

1252   Parry, Hugh J. Dark Road. By James Cross, pseud.

New York: Messner, 1959.
An American lawyer in West Germany is
trapped by circumstances into becoming an undercover agent across the mid-German border.

1253   Payne, Laurence. Spy for Sale. Garden City, N. Y. :
        Doubleday, 1971.
        An underskilled petty thief, upon release from
        jail, is immediately recruited by The Brotherhood
        to hand out religious tracts all over London. One
        day on a corner he is picked up by a glamorous
        girl in a white Aston Martin who insists that some-
        body named Colonel Carruthers needs his assis-
        tance.

1254   Payne, Ronald and John Garrod. The Seventh Fury.
        By John Castle, pseud. New York: Walker, 1963.
        In the best James Bond manner, British Intelli-
        gence pries Dr. Boland away from his London prac-
        tice and sends him deep into the Turkish desert to
        recover a toxic horror.

1255   Pearl, Jack. Our Man Flint. New York: Pinnacle
        Books, 1965. PH
        One day a report comes in to the Zonal Organ-
        ization of World Intelligence and Espionage (ZOWIE
        for short) that three mad scientists, heading up
        their own group called GALAXY, plan to take over
        the world by controlling its weather conditions.
        Chief Dramden of ZOWIE decides that his agent,
        Derek Flint, is the best man to assign on the job
        of halting this dastardly scheme. Armed only with
        his wits and a wonderous cigarette lighter contain-
        ing 83 weapons, Flint trots off on a trail that leads
        to Rome and a small rocky island in the Mediter-
        ranean. This clever take-off on James Bond proved
        a successful motion picture.

1256   _____. The Plot to Kill the President. New
        York: Pinnacle Books, 1970. P

1257   Pearson, John. James Bond: The Authorized Biog-
        raphy of 007. New York: Morrow, 1973.
        Following a fit of depression, Bond is ordered
        by "M" to seek a rest on the island of Bermuda.
        Because of some apparent discrepancies in Mr.
        Fleming's novels, Mr. Pearson is ordered to

interview the noted secret agent and 007 proceeds
to set the record straight.

1258   Pentecost, Hugh. Birthday, Deathday. New York:
        Dodd, Mead, 1972.
            How can a luxury hotel-manager, even with the
        help of the FBI and the CIA, foil the assassin who
        has sworn to kill a guest, Chinese General Ho
        Chang?
            This is part of a longer series on the hotel
        chief most of which are mysteries. One other tale
        with a secret agent bent is:

1259   _____. Golden Trap. New York: Dodd, Mead,
        1967.

1260   Perrault, E. G. Spoil! Garden City, N. Y.: Double-
        day, 1975.
            A tale of murder and intrigue, oil and politics
        in the Canadian Arctic.

1261   _____. The Twelfth Mile. Garden City, N. Y.:
        Doubleday, 1972.
            Sent out of Vancouver to retrieve a large off-
        shore drilling rig, a tugboat skipper finds a crippled
        Russian vessel whose captain has orders not to be
        captured at any cost. Meanwhile the world is on
        the brink of nuclear war.

1262   Perry, Ritchie. The Fall Guy. Boston: Houghton-
        Mifflin, 1972.
            The head of SR(2) has the unhappy job of find-
        ing the source of cocaine being smuggled into
        England from South America. Similar in vein to
        MacLean's Puppet on a Chain (1041).

1263   _____. A Hard Man to Kill. Boston: Houghton-
        Mifflin, 1973.
            An English SR(2) agent is involved in a joint
        effort with the KGB to track down a free-lance
        agent once usefully employed by several countries.

1264   _____. Holiday with a Vengeance. Boston:
        Houghton-Mifflin, 1975.
            British agent Philis must rescue a kidnapped
        consul from a gang of militant rebels in Latin
        America.

1265   _____. Ticket to Ride. Boston: Houghton-Mifflin,
        1974.
        A British agent is assigned to guard a pretty
        widow against the boys of the Mafia and then finds
        out that she is linked to one of its more fantastic
        schemes.

1266   Peters, Brian. The Big H. New York: Holt, 1963.
        An English agent flies to America to help his
        Yankee colleagues frustrate a Soviet plot to smuggle
        huge amounts of heroin into Los Angeles.

1267   Peters, Ellis. The Piper on the Mountain. New
        York: Morrow, 1966.   Y*
        Did British agent Terrell die by accident or
        was he "eliminated" for getting too close to the
        trail of a defector who had stolen some hush-hush
        plane secrets? His step daughter Tossa elects to
        find out and borrowing the cape of Modesty Blaise,
        grimly sets off for Czechoslovakia.

1268   Peters, Ludovic. Riot '71. New York: Walker,
        1967.
        Post-Bondian gore abounds in this British
        thriller recounting Inspector Firth's attempt to find
        mysterious killers inciting riot in the midst of a
        terrible local depression.

1269   _____. Two After Malic. New York: Walker,
        1967.
        A Communist agent is commissioned to return
        escaped scientist Zoran Malic back behind the Iron
        Curtain. When he is thwarted in his first attempt,
        the Red learns the truth of the title. Four other
        excellent suspense-spy stories are:

1270   _____. Cry Vengeance. New York: Walker, 1961.

1271   _____. Double Take. New York: Walker, 1968.

1272   _____. Snatch of Music. New York: Walker, 1962.

1273   _____. Tarakian. New York: Walker, 1963.

1274   Peterson, Paul. The Smugglers. New York: Pocket
        Books, 1974. P
        These are the adventures of Eric Saveman, who
        with his highly-trained superfriends "The Smugglers,"
        goes about busting-up the schemes of sundry nasties.

In this lead story of the series, Saveman and company knock out an enemy's underground spy instal-
lation. Others are:

1275 _____. Mother Luck. New York: Pocket Books,
1974. P

1276 _____. Murder in Blue. New York: Pocket
Books, 1974. P

1277 _____. Tools of the Trade. New York: Pocket
Books, 1974. P
Island dictatorship.

Phillifent, John T., author see Holly, J. Hunter

1278 Picard, Sam. Dead Man Running. New York: Award,
1971. P
These three citations tell of the adventures of
a secret agent group based on tales from a notebook, hence "The Notebook Series."

1279 _____. The Man Who Never Was. New York:
Award, 1971. P

1280 _____. Mission Number One. New York: Award,
1969. P

1281 Pickering, R. E. The Uncommitted Man. New
York: Farrar, Straus & Giroux, 1967.
Dick Philip is one of that mid-1960's LeCarré
school of disillusioned agents. Representing a
business firm in Central Europe, he is caught up
with international intrigue in Vienna.

1282 _____. Himself Again. New York: Farrar,
Straus & Giroux, 1967.
Philip's first adventure.

1283 Pierce, Noel. Messenger from Munich. New York:
Coward-McCann, 1973.
Baron von Gottfried is on a New York mission
that involves him in private revenge and political
assassination on behalf of a neo-Nazi organization
based in Munich.

1284 Pietrkiewicz, Jerzy. Isolation. New York: Holt,
1961.
A free-lance spy uses all of the techniques of

his espionage training to insure the success of his
affair with the wife of a South American diplomat.

1285   Pitts, Denis. This City Is Ours. New York: Mason/
        Charter, 1975.
            Nasties maneuver an oil tanker into New York
        harbor and will blow up Manhattan unless a $130
        billion ransom is paid.

1286   Pollard, Alfred O. A. R. P. Spy. London:
        Hutchinson, 1940.
            In which the agents of British Intelligence dupe
        the Nazis regarding a vital secret early in the war.
        Unless otherwise noted, the following titles by
        Pollard concern British agents vs. Soviets.

1287   _____. Counterfeit Spy. London: Hutchinson,
        1954.
            Our hero is not really an operative, but the
        Russians believe him to be.

1288   _____. The Dead Man's Secret. London: Hutchin-
        son, 1949.

1289   _____. Death Intervened. London: Hutchinson,
        1951.

1290   _____. Death Parade. London: Hutchinson, 1952.

1291   _____. Gestapo Fugitives. London: Hutchinson,
        1944.

1292   _____. The Homicidal Spy. London: Hutchinson,
        1954.
            Is a Soviet villain.

1293   _____. Iron Curtain. London: Hutchinson, 1947.

1294   _____. Red Target. London: Hutchinson, 1952.

1295   _____. Secret Pact. London: Hutchinson, 1940.
        British Intelligence against the Nazis.

1296   _____. Secret Weapon. London: Hutchinson, 1941.
            The Nazis want to snitch a new development in
        British warfare methods.

1297   _____. Wanted by the Gestapo. London: Hutchin-
        son, 1942.
            A variation on 1291.

1298   Pollitz, Edward A. The Forty-First Thief. New

York: Delacorte, 1975.
Big power politics, secret agents, and an attempt by oil suppliers to blackmail the Western
world.

1299   Ponthier, Francois.   Assignment Basra.   New York:
McKay, 1969.
German spy Lt. Richter, right-hand man of
Admiral Canaris, selects Max Wolf, a Jew from
Dachau, for "rehabilitation" and sends him off to
Palestine to spy for the Reich.

1300   Porter, Joyce.   Only with a Bargepole.   New York:
McKay, 1974.   H
Eddie Brown, the world's most reluctant spy
and just about the worst operative ever produced by
British Intelligence, despite his ability to louse up
almost every assignment he is given nevertheless
somehow seems able to accomplish his ends.   Two
other Brown tales are:

1301   _____.   Chinks in the Curtain.   New York: McKay,
1967.   H
Caused by spies getting into Russia.

1302   _____.   Sour Cream with Everything.   New York:
McKay, 1966.   H

1303   Portway, Christopher.   All Exits Barred.   New York:
Pinnacle Books, 1974.   P
Betrayed by British Intelligence and hounded by
Communist pursuers, plucky Tabard and his Czech
fiancée race across Europe to safety in West Berlin.

1304   Powell, Richard P.   All Over but the Shooting.   New
York: Simon & Schuster, 1944.   *
An Arab lady points out German spies in war-
time Washington.

1305   Poyer, Joe.   The Balkan Assignment.   Garden City,
N.Y.:   Doubleday, 1971.   *
A group of neo-Nazis attempt to finance their
current operations from a cache of gold stolen from
the SS at the close of World War II.   A motley
crew of agents, including a former U-boat commander, a Yugoslav partisan, and an American
AAF veteran, is assembled to stop them.

1306 _____. The Chinese Agenda. Garden City, N.Y.:
Doubleday, 1972. *
A team of American and Russian agents, complete with a traitor in their midst, parachutes into
the mountains of Red China to recover a packet of
top secret information from a group of spies.
Their landing is met with a warm surprise.

1307 _____. North Cape. Garden City, N.Y.: Doubleday, 1969. *
A lone pilot is returning from a flight in a
supersonic spy plane over the Russo-Chinese border when he discovers that the Soviets are out to
get him at all cost.

1308 _____. Operation Malacca. Garden City, N.Y.:
Doubleday, 1968. *
A tense Colin Forbes-type adventure set in the
area around Malaya.

1309 Praeger, J. Simon. The Newman Factor. New York:
Dell, 1973. P
A political thriller set in Washington involving
a Russian warhead, the bungled kidnapping of
American scientist Newman, and a cast of spies
and socialites from all over town.

1310 Price, Anthony. The Alamut Ambush. Garden City,
N.Y.: Doubleday, 1972.
Two British agents must foil the plot of Has-
san, head of a fanatical Arab group, who wants no
part in a prospective Arab-Israeli agreement.
[Readers should note that in the matter of the
many volumes unfriendly to the Arab cause, the
sentiments expressed in the annotations reflect only
the intent of the various authors.]

1311 _____. The Alamut Bomb. Garden City, N.Y.:
Doubleday, 1972.
A bomb planted in a car kills a British agent.
A case of mistaken identity? Dr. Audley searches
for the answer and is drawn deep into the activities
of various Palestinian terrorist groups.

1312 _____. Colonel Butler's Wolf. Garden City, N.Y.:
Doubleday, 1972.
When a Soviet agent for some unknown reason

infiltrates Oxford University, Colonel Audley assigns
British operative Jack Butler to find out why.

1313 _____. The Labyrinth Makers. Garden City,
N. Y.: Doubleday, 1971.
Audley is ordered to discover why the Russians
are so interested in an R. A. F. Dakota (DC-3) that
crashed in 1945 and was not discovered until a certain lake was recently drained.

1314 _____. The October Men. .Garden City, N. Y.:
Doubleday, 1974.
While visiting Italy, Dr. Audley is suspected
of defecting; actually he is attempting to plug a
leak in Western security.

1315 _____. Other Paths to Glory. Garden City, N. Y.:
Doubleday, 1975.
Dr. Audley must learn how an obscure World
War I battle threatens today's world.

1316 Priestley, John B. Black-out in Gretley. New York:
Harper, 1952. *
A Canadian double agent is assigned to the little
town of Gretley to plug a damaging leak. He is immediately involved with a bizarre group of men and
women, among whom are Nazi agents stealing secrets.

1317 _____. Saturn over the Water. Garden City,
N. Y.: Doubleday, 1962.
As he searches for the husband of his dying
cousin, a painter uncovers a conspiracy aimed at
world domination and covered by a science institute.

1318 _____. The Shapes of Sleep. Garden City, N. Y.:
Doubleday, 1962.
A British free-lance reporter searches for the
story behind the theft of a piece of green paper.

1319 Puccetti, Roland. Death of the Führer. New York:
St. Martin's, 1973.
A mad assassination attempt on Adolf Hitler.

1320   Quayle, Anthony. <u>On Such a Night</u>. Boston: Little,
        Brown, 1948. *
            A look at the fictional espionage events taking
        place on the British-governed island of Palleria in
        the Mediterranean on the single evening of July 1,
        1942.

1321   Quigley, John. <u>The Last Checkpoint</u>. New York:
        McCall, 1972.
            Walter Eisler, Premier of East Germany, of-
        fers a proposal to the West which includes removal
        of the Berlin Wall. Before proposing this deal,
        however, he had failed to check with Moscow and
        soon finds out that he has created an international
        crisis which may lead to World War III.

1322   _____. <u>The Secret Soldier</u>. New York: New
        American Library, 1966.
            A whisky drummer on Formosa finds himself
        caught up in the smuggling and intrigues of a half-
        caste Chinese friend.

1323   Quinn, Simon. <u>The Devil in Kansas</u>. New York:
        Dell, 1974. P
            This has got to be just about the most prepos-
        terous of all the paperback secret agent-adventurer
        series yet conceived. Ex-CIA agent Frank Kelly
        is an Inquisitor, a member of the Vatican's es-
        pionage agency. As the Pope's hired gun, he is
        the only spy in literature required to do 15 days
        penance after each killing! Others in the Inquisitor
        series thus far are:

1324   _____. <u>His Eminence, Death</u>. New York: Dell,
        1974. P

1325   _____. <u>The Last Time I Saw Hell</u>. New York:
        Dell, 1974. P

1326   _____. <u>Nuplex Red</u>. New York: Dell, 1974. P

1327   Raine, Richard. <u>Bombshell</u>. New York: Harcourt,
        1969.
            The 14th explosion of its kind in Europe claims
        the scientific friend of a British lawyer and indus-
        trialist, David Martini, who then publicly announces

his intention to find whoever is responsible and
draws the appropriate response from the nasties.

1328 _____. The Corder Index. New York: Harcourt,
       1968.
       Martini attempts to find his old acquaintance
       Dick Raine, thriller-writer and compiler of the
       Corder Index, a file containing the scoop on the
       industrial espionage system of the GILA Corpora-
       tion.

1329 _____. Night of the Hawk. New York: Harcourt,
       1968.
       A Swiss banker-diplomat has in his possession
       some highly sensitive evidence which threatens to
       compromise Swiss neutrality. Martini must find
       the man and negotiate a deal enabling the little
       democracy to keep its centuries-old independence.

Ramo, David, pseud. see Divine, Arthur D.

1330 Rascovich, Mark. The Bedford Incident. New York:
       Atheneum, 1963. *
       Comparable to Gallery's The Brink (590), this
       nautical intrigue reveals how the American destroyer
       Bedford cornered a Russian sub in the Arctic.

1331 Rathbone, Julian. Diamonds Bid. New York: Walker,
       1967.
       An enormous bribe changes hands in a Turkish
       Police station and Smollett has the misfortune to
       witness this first step in a vicious power game.

1332 _____. Hand Out. New York: Walker, 1968.
       A British agent stops by Ankara en route to a
       secret assignment on the Turkish frontier. At an
       embassy party, an old friend casually boasts about
       his espionage coups and when he leaves town, our
       hero is not sure whether his cover is still intact.

1333 _____. Kill Cure. New York: St. Martin's Press,
       1975.
       After Claire Mundham signs on as cook to a
       Bangladesh relief expedition, she realizes that not
       only isn't it a mercy mission, but that she is a
       pawn aimed at discrediting a Turkish guerrilla
       movement.

1334 _____. Trip Trap. New York: Putnam, 1972.

1335 _____. With My Knives I Know I'm Good. New
York: Putnam, 1970.
Milyutin defects while visiting Lebanon and is
immediately drawn into the world of espionage
where agents drop one another with regularity and
some even try to get him.

1336 Raven, Simon. Brother Cain. New York: Harper,
1960.

1337 _____. The Sabre Squadron. New York: Harper,
1967. *
In 1952 Daniel Mond, a Cambridge mathemati-
cian, finds the answers to some secret ciphers.
Pursued, he retired to the anonymity of a tradition-
ridden British regiment.

1338 Redgate, John. The Killing Season. New York:
Simon & Schuster, 1967.
A look at the relationship between three U.S.
secret agents operating in East Berlin after one
defects thinking he has eliminated the other two.

Reed, Eliot, pseud. see Ambler, Eric, and
Charles Rodda

1339 Reeman, Doublas. The Deep Silence. New York:
Putnam, 1968. *
The British nuclear submarine Termeraire is
sent to find a damaged American submarine and in
the process runs afoul of the Chinese Communists.

1340 Reynolds, Philip. When and If. Transl. from French
by Joseph F. McCrindle. New York: Duell, 1952.
An R.A.F. intelligence agent sets up a spy
network during a supposed future war between the
West and Soviet Russia.

1341 Richards, Clay. The Gentle Assassins. Indianapolis:
Bobbs-Merrill, 1964. *
Lt. Col. Kim Lock of the U.S. Army is assigned, along with his canine helper "Dante," to
help the CIA get two State Department defectors out
of Cuba.

1342   Richards, Paul. Moscow at Noon Is the Target. New
        York: Award, 1973. P
            A new "Hotline Espionage" series which features
        "detente" between Soviet and Western agents. In
        this episode, the two sides work to head off a mad-
        man who has our title in mind.

1343   _____. One of Our Spacecraft Is Missing. New
        York: Award, 1973. P

1344   _____. The President Has Been Kidnapped. New
        York: Award, 1973. P

1345   Ritner, Peter. Red Carpet for the Shah. New York:
        Morrow, 1975.
            What happens when the leader of Iran tries to
        take over the world?

        Roberts, James H. see Duncan, Robert L.

1346   Roberts, Jan. The Judas Sheep. New York: Satur-
        day Review Press, 1975.
            CIA agent MacDonald asks an art dealer to
        check out artist Stavros, who belongs to a left-wing
        organization.

1347   Roberts, Katherine E. Center of the Web. Garden
        City, N.Y.: Doubleday, 1942.
            A trained but amateur British spy is sent to
        the House on Harmony Street, in occupied Antwerp,
        to break-up the web of agents headed by the Frau-
        lein Doktor. Serialized in Liberty Magazine.

1348   Roberts, Thomas A. The Heart of the Dog. New
        York: Random House, 1972.
            A former CIA linguist accepts a Mideast courier
        job from "the company."

1349   Robinson, Derek. Rotten with Honour. New York:
        Viking, 1973.
            A young British banker who does a bit of moon-
        lighting as a spy must beat an old Russian master
        agent to the recovery of a nuclear scientist who
        has discovered a new weapon.

1350   Rogers, Ray M. The Negotiator. New York: David
        McKay, 1975.
            Is the Secretary of State playing a double game?

1351   Romano, Deane. Flight from Time One. New York:
        Walker, 1972.
            In which another nasty is appropriately handled
        by the boys from Britain's MI6.

1352   Roos, Audrey and William. A Few Days in Madrid.
        New York: Scribner's, 1965.
            Chosen to escort a 12-year-old boy to Spain,
        a legal secretary finds herself enmeshed in es-
        pionage, an assassination plot, and other grisly
        nasties.

1353   Rosenberger, Joseph. The Castro File. New York:
        Pinnacle Books, 1974. P
            Master of disguise, deception, and destruction,
        Richard Camellion is called in whenever the local
        authorities and the CIA are stumped. Well does
        he deserve his name, "The Death Merchant."
            In this story, he must prevent a battle for
        power between the Cubans and the Russians in a
        plot which includes the elimination of Castro and
        his replacement with a look-alike Russian stooge.
        Other tales in this exclusively paperback series
        are:

1354   _____. The Albanian Connection. New York:
        Pinnacle Books, 1973. P

1355   _____. The Billionaire Mission. New York:
        Pinnacle Books, 1974. P

1356   _____. The Chinese Conspiracy. New York:
        Pinnacle Books, 1973. P

1357   _____. The Death Merchant. New York: Pinnacle
        Books, 1971. P

1358   _____. The Laser War. New York: Pinnacle
        Books, 1974. P

1359   _____. Operation Overkill. New York: Pinnacle
        Books, 1972. P

1360   _____. The Psychotran Plot. New York: Pin-
        nacle Books, 1972. P

1361   _____. Satan Strike. New York: Pinnacle Books,
        1973. P

1362   Rosenblum, Robert. The Mushroom Cave. Garden
        City, N.Y.: Doubleday, 1973.

A student radical attempting to smuggle a revolutionary manuscript out of Russia is caught and
when the news breaks in the West, he becomes a
pawn in a ruthless game between the Soviets and
the CIA.

1363   Rosenhaupt, Hans. The True Deceivers. New York:
        Dodd, Mead, 1954.
        A German-born OSS officer works for the
        American army interrogating Nazi POWs during the
        war.

1364   Ross, Regina. Falls the Shadow. New York: Dela-
        corte, 1974.
        A British Intelligence agent has been kidnapped
        by a French Communist underground gang and is
        being tortured to reveal the whereabouts of a price-
        less Holy Crown. In the background are two KGB
        agents waiting to snitch both the agent and the
        Crown in order to embarrass Britain at a forth-
        coming peace conference. The chase covers most
        of Europe.

1365   Rossiter, John. The Deadly Gold. New York:
        Walker, 1975.
        A British agent infiltrates a gang planning to
        steal a priceless gold statue from Spain.

1366   _____. The Deadly Green. New York: Walker, 1971.
        A now-and-then agent for the Directorate of
        British Special Services must locate a man from
        the Foreign Office who has vanished with one
        million pounds.

1367   _____. A Rope for General Dietz. New York:
        Walker, 1972.

1368   Rostand, Robert. The Killer Elite. New York:
        Delacorte, 1973.
        An expendable spy is unofficially assigned to
        protect a deposed prime minister from assassina-
        tion.

1369   _____. The Viper's Game. New York: Delacorte,
        1974.
        Mike Lochen, ex-CIA man, must get 50 people
        off the Portugese island colony of São Tome--or at

least keep them one step ahead of machete -carrying, white -hating native tribesmen!

1370 Rosten, Leo. A Most Private Intrigue. New York: Atheneum, 1967.
Galton goes to Istanbul to help obtain three Western scientists from behind the Iron Curtain; falls in love.

1371 Roth, Holly. The Van Dreisen Affair. New York: Random House, 1960.
Our heroine, Elena van Wreisen, effects the escape of a professed Communist, is distrusted upon her return to America, and produces an over -all action designed to protect American citizens. Other yarns include:

1372 _____. Content Assignment. New York: Random House, 1954.

1373 _____. Mask of Glass. New York: Random House, 1954.

1374 _____. The Sleeper. New York: Random House, 1955.

1375 Rothberg, Abraham. The Heirs of Cain. New York: Putnam, 1967.
Via flashbacks, in which he recounts his mis- sion to liquidate a pair of ex-Nazi scientists work- ing for Egypt, Nissim reveals how he became the "Sword" of Israeli Intelligence and the "Heir of Cain."

1376 _____. The Stalking Horse. New York: Saturday Review Press, 1972.
Years ago at the American embassy in Moscow, Chapman knew a Russian playwright KGB agent named Federov. Now after his retirement to a farm, the CIA asks him to hide a Russian defector who turns out to be Alex. The peace is broken when the remote farm hideout is discovered by Soviet agents bent on homicide.

1377 _____. The Thousand Doors. New York: Putnam, 1965.

1378 Rothwell, Henry T. Duet for Three Spies. New York: Roy, 1967.

Michael Brooks is sent by "the company" to
rescue a secret geological survey team in the
Congo which is under attack by guerrillas and
which has a Belgian spy in its midst.

1379   _____. No Honour Amongst Spies. New York:
Roy, 1969.
Agent Brooks is hustled off to Rhodesia to rescue Deidre Page from the horrors of a Russian exchange. With both his own people and the KGB
after him, Brooks has the certain knowledge that
success will end his career--if a bullet doesn't
first! Two more Brooks titles are:

1380   _____. Dive Deep for Danger. New York: Roy,
1966.

1381   _____. Exit of a Spy. New York: Roy, 1969.

1382 Royce, Kenneth. Code Name: Woodcutter. New
York: Simon & Schuster, 1975.
The seizure of a London hospital by five men
assumes international proportions upon the discovery
that the U.S. Secretary of State is a patient therein.

1383   _____. My Turn to Die. New York: Simon &
Schuster, 1958.

Rubinstein, Paul, coauthor see Tanous, Peter

1384 Rumanes, George N. The Man with the Black Worry-
beads. New York: Dutton, 1973.
A group of undercover fighters in wartime
Athens are called upon to keep a convoy of ships
from reaching Rommel's forces in North Africa.

1385 Ryack, Francis. Green Light, Red Catch. Transl.
from French by Gordon Latta. New York: Stein
& Day, 1973.
Russian space scientist Kazienko, vacationing
at a Crimean beach resort, is snitched by British
secret agents on behalf of Israel. Then it is the
turn of Soviet operatives to try and get him back.

1386   _____. Loaded Gun. Transl. from French by
Norman Dale. New York: Stein & Day, 1972.
Yako, a Soviet spy, is captured by the British
and later released. Unbeknownst to him, the

Limeys have attached a tracking device on him
which leads to a chase through the French and
Spanish countrysides.

1387 _____. Woman Hunt. Transl. from the French.
New York: Stein & Day, 1972.
Dominique has no idea that her husband is a
spy. When she catches him in bed with another
beauty (there are no homely girls in spy stories!),
the gun in her hand goes off and he is dead. Not
knowing that he was actually "on business," she
runs--pursued by French and Russian agents who
want to silence her for what they believe she knows
of her ex's espionage knowledge.

1388 Ryder, Jonathan. The Cry of the Halidon. New
York: Delacorte, 1974.
An American geologist doing a secret survey
of the island of Jamaica finds himself the pawn of
British Intelligence and even his own team members.

1389 Sager, Gordon. The Formula. Philadelphia: Lippincott, 1952.
A secret formula is hidden somewhere among
the art treasures of Venice and agents from everywhere want to get their hands on it.

1390 St. George, Geoffrey. The Proteus Pact. Boston:
Little, Brown, 1975.
A German scientist, revolted by the Nazis,
works secretly for British Intelligence on a new
superalloy.

St. John, David, pseud. see Hunt, E. Howard

1391 Sale, Richard. For the President's Eyes Only. New
York: Simon & Schuster, 1971.
American electronics expert Carson is "trans-
formed" into millionaire Simon Kincade and then
loaned to British Intelligence for "Operation Key-
hole," a plan to eliminate an international band of
extortioners working out of London.

1392 Salinger, Pierre. The Lollipop Republic. Garden
City, N.Y.: Doubleday, 1971.
During a Latin American revolution in the

1980's, America sits by until it is too late.

1393 _____. On Instructions of My Government. Garden City, N. Y. : Doubleday, 1971.
President Kennedy's press secretary's first
novel involves an American president in a crisis
similar to the October 1962 Cuban Missile Crisis.

1394 Sandulescu, Jacques, and Annie Gottlieb. The Carpathian Caper. New York: Putnam, 1975.
A colorful band of adventurers join forces in
Transylvania to pull off the heist of a $5-million
art treasure hidden in a monastery high in the
forbidding Carpathian mountains.

1395 Sangster, James. Foreign Exchange. New York:
Norton, 1972.
The hero of Private I (1396) is sent to Russia
posing as a tractor salesman in order to carry off
an ultra secret mission.

1396 _____. Private I. New York: Norton, 1967.
A spy yarn in which our hero crisscrosses
several continents secure in his belief that he has
finally escaped the usual fate of Max agents who
desert "The Agency." Unfortunately for him, his
conscience suckers him into stopping off to help
his ex-wife divorce her current husband--and BANG!

1397 _____. Touchfeather. New York: Norton, 1969.
Katy Touchfeather is an airline hostess with a
difference--she is a Modesty Blaise-style secret
agent who hops around the globe carrying out the
assignments of her employer, Whithall's mysterious
Mr. Blaser. Two other Touchfeather works are:

1398 _____. Touch Gold. New York: Norton, 1970.

1399 _____. Touchfeather Too. New York: Norton,
1970.
Sequel to no. 1397.

1400 Sapir, Richard and Warren Murphy. The Last War
Dance. New York: Pinnacle Books, 1974. P
C. U. R. E. , the world's most secret crime and
spying organization, created the perfect weapon--
Remo Williams--a man programmed to become a
cold calculating death machine and codenamed "The

Destroyer." In this tale, Remo must deliver a
monument, which the Revolutionary Indian Party
wishes destroyed and which masks the Cassandra,
an atomic doomsday machine.

1401 _____. The Terror Squad. New York: Pinnacle
Books, 1973. P
"The Destroyer," must prevent the formation
of an international gang of outlaws--skyjackers,
racists, guerrillas, mercenaries--from being formed
and holding the world to ransom. Other "Destroyer"
titles in this exclusively paperback series are:

1402 _____. Acid Rock. New York: Pinnacle Books,
1974. P

1403 _____. The Chinese Puzzle. New York: Pinnacle Books, 1972. P

1404 _____. Created, The Destroyer. New York:
Pinnacle Books, 1971. P

1405 _____. Death Check. New York: Pinnacle Books,
1972. P

1406 _____. Death Therapy. New York: Pinnacle
Books, 1972. P

1407 _____. Dr. Quake. New York: Pinnacle Books,
1972. P

1408 _____. Funny Money. New York: Pinnacle Books,
1975. P

1409 _____. Judgment Day. New York: Pinnacle
Books, 1974. P

1410 _____. Kill or Cure. New York: Pinnacle Books,
1973. P

1411 _____. Mafia Fix. New York: Pinnacle Books,
1972. P

1412 _____. Murder Ward. New York: Pinnacle
Books, 1974. P

1413 _____. Murderer's Shield. New York: Pinnacle
Books, 1973. P

1414 _____. Oil Slick. New York: Pinnacle Books,
1974. P

1415 _____. Slave Safari. New York: Pinnacle Books,
1973. P

1416   _____. Summit Chase. New York: Pinnacle
          Books, 1973. P

1417   _____. Union Bust. New York: Pinnacle Books,
          1973. P

1418   Saturday Evening Post, Editors of. Danger: Great
          Stories of Mystery and Suspense. Garden City,
          N. Y. : Doubleday, 1967.
              Contains several spy novelettes by, among
          others, Ian Fleming.

1419   Scott, Virgil and Dominic Koski. The Kreutzman
          Formula. New York: Simon & Schuster, 1974.
              Professor Kregg is sent off to Jamaica with an
          important formula in his notes in a desperate ploy
          by British counter-intelligence to catch a spy known
          only as Aristotle.

1420   Seaman, Donald. The Bomb that Could Lip Read.
          New York: Stein & Day, 1974.
              Kelly, the world's highest paid mercenary,
          must create and plant a bomb that conveys to its
          detonator the best time for the blast. British
          Major Welbourne is determined to stop both Kelly
          and his plaything.

1421   Searls, Hank. Pentagon. New York: Geis, 1972.
              Colonel Lee Frost of Counter-Intelligence is
          assigned to see who took a pot-shot at the window
          of the Chief of the officially-abolished Chemico-
          Biological Warfare Division of the Pentagon. En
          route to solving that mystery, he encounters three
          more.

1422   Sela, Owen. The Bearer Plot. New York: Pantheon,
          1973.
              A young pilot-cum-spy is involved with the im-
          famous ODESSA in a deal concerning the sale of
          some valuable stamps to a Spanish nobleman front-
          ing for the group.

1423   _____. The Portugese Fragment. New York:
          Pantheon, 1973.
              Agreeing to visit Asia for a bit of "harmless
          smuggling," Maaston ends up battling the nasties
          for a treasure off the coast of Ceylon.

1424   Semprun, Jorge. The Second Death of Ramon Mer-
        cader. Transl. from French by Len Ortzen. New
        York: Grove Press, 1973.
                A mysterious agent of some unknown govern-
        ment arrives in Amsterdam and soon runs afoul of
        the Dutch, Russians, East Germans, and the Amer-
        ican intelligence boys.

1425   _____. Prayer for an Assassin. Transl. from
        French by Cornelia Schaeffer. Garden City, N. Y.:
        Doubleday, 1960.
                Mark Vargas is in the post-war city of Buda-
        pest with orders to kill a high Communist official.

1426   Seth, Ronald. Operation Getaway. New York: John
        Day, 1954.
                British agents are parachuted behind the Iron
        Curtain to rescue an important Communist prisoner.
        Others include:

1427   _____. In the Nude. New York· John Day, 1955.

1428   _____. The Patriot. New York: John Day, 1954.

1429   _____. A Spy Has No Friends. New York: John
        Day, 1952.

1430   Seward, Jac. The Cave of the Chinese Skeletons.
        Rutland, Vt.: Tuttle, 1964.
                British agent Curt Stone, a James Bond type
        in the Far East, battles Communist operatives to
        find the vital Izu cache. Two other Stone stories
        are:

1431   _____. Eurasian Virgins. Rutland, Vt.: Tuttle,
        1968.

1432   _____. Frogman Assassination. Rutland, Vt.:
        Tuttle, 1968.

1433   Shapiro, Lionel. Torch for a Dark Journey. Garden
        City, N. Y.: Doubleday, 1950.
                The lives of an American oil tycoon, a Hun-
        garian adventurer, an American reporter, a Czech
        scientist and a Czech Communist all interweave in
        this tale of post-war intrigue.

1434   Shaw, Bynum. The Sound of Small Hammers. New
        York: Morrow, 1962.

One man's attempt to privately subsidize a
propaganda operation in East Germany.

1435   Sheckley, Robert.   Dead Run.   New York: Dial Press,
        1961.

1436   _____.   The Game of X.   New York: Dial Press,
        1966.
            William Nye is invited by a friend to help trap
        a Russian spy.

1437   Sheehan, Edward R. F.   Kingdom of Illusion.   New
        York: Random House, 1964.
            The sleepy Arab nation of Al Khadra becomes
        a strategic Cold War pawn between Russia and
        America.

1438   Sheldon, Walter J.   Gold Bait.   Greenwich, Conn. :
        Fawcett, 1973.   P

1439   _____.   Yellow Music Kill.   Greenwich, Conn. :
        Fawcett, 1974.   P
            Matt Larkin, vice-president of a boat company,
        agrees to do a little undercover work when he goes
        to China to help their Olympic yachting team.

1440   Sherlock, John.   The Ordeal of Major Grigsby.   New
        York: Morrow, 1964.
            A retired British guerrilla leader is asked to
        return to Malaya and destroy Chen Tak, a young
        Chinese insurgent he had trained to fight against
        the Japanese.

1441   Sherwood, John.   Ambush for Anatol.   Garden City,
        N. Y. :   Doubleday, 1953.
            An unwholesome figure known only as Anatol
        who seems to be able to get the goods on all sorts
        of important people and drive them into helping him
        in a currency exchange racket, gets knocked off;
        the British agent on his trail is now forced to
        change gears and pursue the figure who takes over
        the business.

1442   _____.   Mr. Blessington's Imperialist Plot.   Gar-
        den City, N. Y. :   Doubleday, 1951.   H
            Mild-mannered Mr. Blessington of the British
        Treasury journeys to a Balkan country and manages

to get himself kidnapped.   A British Intelligence
agent is then sent in to rescue him from his Soviet
abductors.

1443   _____.   Two Die in Singapore.   Garden City, N. Y. :
Doubleday, 1954.
Another twisting spy story in which both the
hero and villain "buy it" in the end.

1444   Sigel, Efrem.   The Kermanschah Transfer.   New
York: Macmillan, 1973.
Harold Kiels, an American engineer in Iran,
is recruited by Israeli agents to see that a shipment of arms is delivered to the Kurds, who are
fighting the Iraqui.

1445   Silone, Ignazio.   The Fox and the Camellias.   Transl.
from Italian by Eric Mosbacher.   New York: Harper, 1961.
Another of those spy romances.   At a Swiss
farm near Brissago our heroine maintains a secret
outpost for the wartime Italian underground.

1446   Simmel, Johannes M.   Dear Fatherland.   Transl.
from German by Richard and Clara Winston.   New
York: Random House, 1969.
Set in the Berlin of the recent past, this German spy thriller concerns a sometime burglar who
is involved in a plot to kidnap a man who bankrolls
freedom tunnels from the East.

1447   _____.   It Can't Always Be Caviar: The Fabulously
Daring Adventures of an Involuntary Secret Agent.
Garden City, N, Y. : Doubleday, 1965.   H
A comic spy caper involving the 25-year service of an agent who made friends, swapped information, and never missed a chance to increase his
savings account!

1448   Simmons, Geoffrey.   The Z-Papers.   New York:
Arbor House, 1975.
Someone is trying to kill the U. S. Defense
Secretary.

1449   Simmons, Mary K.   The Year of the Rooster.   New
York: Delacorte, 1971.
While visiting Tokyo, Eliot is impressed into

the service of American Intelligence to find a stolen
list of enemy operatives obtained by his predecessor
--who was killed trying to hang onto it.

1450   Simpson, Howard R.   The Three-Day Alliance.   Gar-
        den City, N.Y.: Doubleday, 1971.
            Soviet and British intelligence operatives team
        up in a three-day effort to block a Chinese attempt
        at establishing a power base somewhere in conti-
        nental Europe.

1451   Sinclair, Michael.   The Dollar Covenant.   New York:
        Norton, 1973.
            When the government of Scotland goes bankrupt,
        an agency known as The Federation of American
        Caledonian Societies literally takes over the country
        and turns it into a totalitarian state.   This leaves
        Mockinham no choice but to plot its overthrow.

1452   _____.   Folio Forty One.   New York: Putnam,
        1972.
            Agent MacCraig is assigned to investigate a
        Scotch organization called "The Norsemen," con-
        spiring to set up a new nation made up of Scan-
        dinavia and Scotland.

1453.   _____.   Sonntag.   New York: Putnam, 1971.
            British operative Sonntag comes unexpectedly to
        public view with the discovery of some bodies on
        the western border of Berlin.

1454   Sinclair, Upton B.   Dragon Harvest.   New York:
        Viking, 1945.
            Presidential secret agent Lanny Budd gathers
        intelligence in Vichy France and Germany from the
        likes of Goering and Hitler himself.   Sequel to
        Presidential Agent (1457).

1455   _____.   O Shepherd, Speak.   New York: Viking,
        1949.
            Lanny Budd's adventures are chronicled through
        the end of the war and take him to Nuremburg for
        the war crimes trials and on to Russia as Presi-
        dent Truman's personal agent to Stalin.   Sequel to
        One Clear Call (1456).

1456   _____.   One Clear Call.   New York: Viking, 1948.

As President Roosevelt's personal agent, Budd
operates in Italy, France, Germany, and Spain.
In Germany, he poses as a friend to top Nazis; in
France, as an advisor to the forces defending Normandy. Sequel to Presidential Mission (1458).

1457 _____. Presidential Agent. New York: Viking,
1944.
Because of his life-time intimacy with men in
the news, FDR chooses Budd to be his personal
secret agent. In this work, Budd looks into the
plots and counter-plots undertaken by the Axis in
the period between Munich and Pearl Harbor.

1458 _____. Presidential Mission. New York: Viking,
1947.
Budd is sent to North Africa to talk with the
French before the 1942 Allied invasion and then
moves on to Germany gathering all kinds of information useful to the Allies. Sequel to The World
to Win (1460).

1459 _____. The Return of Lanny Budd. New York:
Viking, 1953.
In this last of a series, our hero is called out
of retirement to become involved in the various
crises of 1946-1949, including the spy trial of his
sister.

1460 _____. The World to Win. New York: Viking,
1946.
In this sequel to Dragon Harvest (1454), agent
Budd continues his Presidential espionage, visiting
Vichy France for a talk with Pierre Laval and
Russia for a conversation with Stalin.

1461 Singer, Sally M. For Dying You Always Have Time.
New York: Putnam, 1971.
Sydelle abandons the regular tour of Italy to
deliver a corpse as a favor for her lover which
gets her drawn into the Mideast crisis and the hunt
for an unknown secret weapon.

1462 Slappey, Sterling. Exodus of the Damned. New
York: New American Library, 1968.
A look at how a group of ex-Nazis bribed a
Jew to smuggle 500 war criminals from Germany

to an enclave in South America.

1463   Slater, Humphrey. Conspirator. New York: Har-
       court, 1948.
       What happens when a British soldier in the pay
       of the Communists as a spy marries a loyal Eng-
       lish lass.

1464   Smith, Don. Secret Mission: Angola. New York:
       Award, 1971. P
       In this Nick Carter-Sam Durell style action
       series, our hero, Phil Sherman, is called upon to
       smash sundry nasties in the name of American
       freedom, independence, and liberty. In this ac-
       count, he must do in some terrible fellows ferment-
       ing a dastardly scheme in the huge Portugese colony
       in Africa. Other titles in this exclusively paper-
       back series include:

1465   _____. Secret Mission: Athens. New York:
       Award, 1973. P
       Neo-Nazi group plans a coup against the Greek
       government.

1466   _____. Secret Mission: Cairo. New York:
       Award, 1974. P

1467   _____. Secret Mission: Corsica. New York:
       Award, 1973. P
       An evil genius plans to kill a million Americans.

1468   _____. Secret Mission: Corsican Takeover. New
       York: Award, 1974. P

1469   _____. Secret Mission: Death Stalk in Spain.
       New York: Award, 1972. P

1470   _____. Secret Mission: Haitian Vendetta. New
       York: Award, 1973. P

1471   _____. Secret Mission: Istanbul. New York:
       Award, 1972. P

1472   _____. Secret Mission: The Kremlin Plot. New
       York: Award, 1971. P

1473   _____. Secret Mission: The Libyan Contract.
       New York: Award, 1974. P

1474   _____. Secret Mission: The Marseilles Enforcer.
       New York: Award, 1974. P

1475 _____. Secret Mission: Morocco. New York:
Award, 1974. P

1476 _____. Secret Mission: Munich. New York:
Award, 1970. P

1477 _____. Secret Mission: The Night of the Assassin.
New York: Award, 1973. P

1478 _____. Secret Mission: North Korea. New York:
Award, 1970. P

1479 _____. Secret Mission: The Padrone. New York:
Award, 1971. P

1480 _____. Secret Mission: The Payoff. New York:
Award, 1973. P

1481 _____. Secret Mission: Peking. New York:
Award, 1973. P
A computer designed to destroy Chinese nuclear
potential develops kinks at the last minute.

1482 _____. Secret Mission: Prague. New York:
Award, 1974. P
A Black Power rebellion is fueled with secret
arms.

1483 _____. Secret Mission: Tibet. New York:
Award, 1969. P

1484 Snelling, Laurence. The Heresy. New York: Norton, 1973.
When a film company decides to record the
true-life adventures of a French Resistance outfit,
its efforts are sabotaged by veterans still in business, knocking out excessively repressive governments of the left and right.

1485 Spillane, Frank M. The By-Pass Control. By
Mickey Spillane, pseud. New York: Dutton, 1966.
Tiger Mann of the secret Martin Grady Organization must save the world from nuclear holocaust
by finding a missing scientist who specializes in the
miniaturization of equipment and thus has found a
way to by-pass presidential control of America's
doomsday arsenal.

1486 _____. Day of the Guns. By Mickey Spillane,
pseud. New York: Dutton, 1965.
Agent Mann discovers an old flame who had

shot him, leaving him for dead in Austria just before the end of the war. Promising to "take care"
of her, he finds a major Communist conspiracy is
more pressing and thus he must "take care" of it
first. As the old adage goes, "business before
pleasure!"

1487 _____. The Delta Factor. By Mickey Spillane,
pseud. New York: Dutton, 1965.
        Recaptured after his attempt to flee a maximum
security prison, Morgan is offered a deal: return
to jail or take on a little special mission in the
Caribbean.

1488 _____. The Girl Hunters. By Mickey Spillane,
pseud. New York: Dutton, 1963.
        To avenge the death of a girlfriend, Mike
Hammer must take on a Communist spy ring and
a master killer known only as The Dragon. Two
others are:

1489 _____. Bloody Sunrise. By Mickey Spillane,
pseud. New York: Dutton, 1965.

1490 _____. Death Dealers. By Mickey Spillane,
pseud. New York: Dutton, 1965.

1491 Stackleborg, Gene. Double Agent. New York: Popular Library, 1959. P
        Discredited CIA agent Bill Maclean joins a
friend in a plot to capture a Soviet spy, turn him
over to the Intelligence boys, and take a big reward. The only problem is that the Russian in
question doesn't want to play along!

1492 Stanford, Alfred. The Mission in Sparrow Bush
Lane. New York: Morrow, 1963.
        In 1943 London, German agents are trying to
penetrate the secrets of the "Mulberry" artificial
harbors to be used in the 1944 D-Day landings at
Normandy.

1493 Stanton, Ken. Cold Blue Death. New York: MacFadden-
Bartell, 1970. P
        In this nautical spy series, a secret organization
known as the Aquanauts operates out of the Navy department under the leadership of a crusty old admiral responsible only to the Chief of Naval

Operations and the President. Its chief agent is
Lt. Cmdr. William Martin, a superior diver known
as "The Tiger Shark," who can usually be found
either chasing the girls or boating about in the
ultra-secret mini-submarine in which he performs
all of his missions. In this story, the Aquanauts
are once again pitted against their chief enemy,
the infamous double-dealing Russians. Others are:

1494 _____. Evil Cargo. New York: MacFadden-Bartell, 1973. P

1495 _____. Operation Deep Six. New York: MacFadden-
Bartell, 1972. P

1496 _____. Operation Mermaid. New York: MacFadden-
Bartell, 1974. P

1497 _____. Operation Sea Monster. New York:
MacFadden-Bartell, 1974. P
A mysterious sea creature seems to be doing
naughty things to innocent seafarers.

1498 _____. Operation Steelfish. New York: MacFadden-
Bartell, 1972. P

1499 _____. Sargasso Secret. New York: MacFadden-
Bartell, 1971. P
What is really causing all those mysterious
disappearances in "The Devil's Triangle" ... ?

1500 _____. Seek, Strike, and Destroy! New York:
MacFadden-Bartell, 1971. P

1501 _____. Stalkers of the Sea. New York: MacFadden-
Bartell, 1972. P
Martin vs. the James Bond of the Russian es-
pionage establishment.

1502 _____. Ten Seconds to Zero. New York:
MacFadden-Bartell, 1970. P
The Aquanauts must locate the deadly new Rus-
sian underwater missile being deployed against
American nuclear submarines.

1503 _____. Whirlwind Beneath the Sea. New York:
MacFadden-Bartell, 1972. P
Who is behind the unnatural eruption that rose
from the seabed of the Indian Ocean and killed a
half million Bengalis.... ?

1504 Stapp, Robert. A More Perfect Union. New York:

Harper, 1970.
Growing up in a divided America, a Southerner
finds that he is the man tapped to assassinate the
nefarious President Spearman of the Confederate
States of America. Shades of George Orwell,
James Bond, and "Mission Impossible."

1505   Stark, Richard. The Blackbird. New York:
       Macmillan, 1969.
       Alan Grofield, actor, thief, and agent for the
secret government agency called "Brand X," is
sent off to a conference in Quebec, where he tan-
gles with the beautiful and menacing lady spy,
Vivian Kamdela from Undurwa.

Steel, Kurt, pseud. see Kagley, Rudolf

1506   Stein, Aaron M. The Finger. Garden City, N.Y.:
       Doubleday, 1973.
       The dangerous game of smuggling scientific
"brains" from behind the Iron Curtain engulfs Matt
Erridge, a "visitor" to Karlsbad, Czechoslovakia.

1507   Stern, Richard M. I Hide, We Seek. New York:
       Scribner's, 1966.
       Before leaving America to turn over an inven-
tion which the government will not allow him to
make public, a scientist, intent upon defection to
a more "understanding" nation, falls in love with
an American girl agent.

1508   _____. In Any Case. New York: McGraw-Hill,
       1963.
       A father fights to clear his son of treason
charges emanating from his failure in working with
an underground group in Western Europe during
World War II.

1509   _____. The Kessler Legacy. New York: Scrib-
       ner's, 1967.

1510   _____. The Search for Tabatha Carr. New York:
       Scribner's, 1960.
       Willard Robbins searches across Europe for a
girl who stands to gain a cool one million dollars
if she can be found in time.

1511   Stevenson, Dorothy E.   Crooked Adam.   New York:
        Rinehart, 1942.   *
            A crippled British schoolmaster helps break up
        a Nazi ring attempting to circumvent all inventions
        of value to Britain's war effort.

1512   Stewart, Edward.   They've Shot the President's
        Daughter.   Garden City, N. Y. :   Doubleday, 1973.
            When the President visits his home town to lay
        a wreath at the grave of his parents, someone kills
        his daughter.   Why?   Was the assassin just a poor
        shot or was the girl really the target?

1513   Stewart, John I. M.   Man from the Sea.   By Michael
        Innes, pseud.   New York: Dodd, Mead, 1955.
            A man of deep mystery possessing scientific
        knowledge which can endanger world peace is the
        principal quarry in a chase-filled novel which em-
        ploys almost every sort of vehicle known in the
        United Kingdom, from "chopper" to ambulance.

1514   Stimson, Robert G. and James Bellah.   The Avenger
        Tapes.   New York: Pinnacle Books, 1971.   P
            Agent Case must find a set of stolen tapes
        which show the route patterns for the experimental
        Avenger missile.

1515   Stokes, Donald H.   Captive in the Night.   New York:
        Coward-McCann, 1951.
            An American ex-soldier finds himself wrapped
        up in a post-war tale of intrigue in French-occupied
        Algeria.

1516   Stone, David.   The Tired Spy.   New York: Putnam,
        1962.
            Paul Porlock, agent 776H of MI-13 British
        Counter-Intelligence, has gone on vacation to Italy
        to escape his harried home life.   The only problem
        is that the intelligence community does not believe
        that he is simply on a holiday.

        Stratton, Thomas, author   see   Holly, J. Hunter

        Stuart, Ian, pseud.   see   MacLean, Alistair

1517   Stuart, Warren.   The Sword and the Net.   New York:
        Morrow, 1941.   *

The love of an American girl causes a Nazi
spy to change sides.

1518   Sulzberger, C. L. The Tooth Merchant. Chicago:
       Quadrangle Books, 1973.
           Starting out ugly, this tale portrays an Ar-
       menian crook who uncovers an astonishing secret
       and attempts to sell it to world leaders in 1953.

1519   Swiggett, Howard. The Hidden and the Hunted. New
       York: Morrow, 1951.
           An American spy battles a Russian agent for
       the recovery and possession of the papers of a
       Czech economist.

1520   Tack, Alfred. The Spy Who Wasn't Exchanged. Gar-
       den City, N. Y.: Doubleday, 1969.
           In Moscow James Mason and Anne Blane find
       out they have to play both sides of the espionage
       game.

1521   Tanous, Peter and Paul Rubinstein. The Petrodollar
       Takeover. New York: Putnam, 1975.
           Oil-rich Arabs attempt to purchase General
       Motors.

1522   Teilhet, Darwin and Hildegarde. Double Agent. New
       York: Coward-McCann, 1945.

1523   _____ and _____. Rim of Terror. New York:
       Coward-McCann, 1950.
           En route to Seattle, Elizabeth Whitehill picks
       up a man and becomes involved with a group of
       alien agents attempting to capture her rider for a
       mock trial to be held in an unnamed totalitarian
       country.

1524   Templeton, Charles. The Kidnapping of the President.
       New York: Simon & Schuster, 1975.
           The U.S. President is captured by a gang of
       Latin American revolutionaries.

1525   Thayer, Charles W. Checkpoint. New York: Harper,
       1964.
           Harry Harding, deputy to U.S. Rep. Schuyler,

becomes involved in Soviet-American military intrigue and a German underground activity which
blows up into a crisis at the Berlin Wall.

1526   _____. Moscow Interlude. New York: Harper,
            1962.
            A tale of espionage and intrigue centering
around an American attaché and his Russian wife,
whose brother has met a strange death for reasons
not given by Soviet authorities.

1527 Thomas, Leslie. Orange Wednesday. New York:
            Delacorte, 1968.
            When U.S., British, French, German, and
Russian leaders plan to meet and sign a treaty
unifying both Germanys, certain nasties conspire
to prevent the agreement.

1528 Thomas, Ross. The Backup Men. New York: Mor-
            row, 1971. H
            The further adventures of Padilo and McCorkle,
who act as "backup men" for a twin pair of famous
British espionage agents.

1529   _____. Cast a Yellow Shadow. New York: Mor-
            row, 1967. H
            More McCorkle action.

1530   _____. The Cold War Swap. New York: Morrow,
            1966. H
            Mac McCorkle, a barkeep in West Berlin, has
a partner named Michael Padilo, who uses the job
as a cover for his espionage activities. When
Washington decides to sacrifice Padilo to recover a
pair of defectors, McCorkle must go to his friend's
aid.

1531   _____. The Fools in Town Are on Our Side. New
            York: Morrow, 1971. H
            The director of U.S. intelligence in the Far
East "retires" and upon returning home, becomes
involved in a municipal election.

1532   _____. The Singapore Wink. New York: Morrow,
            1969.
            Hollywood stunt man is up for an assignment to
Malaya.

1533   _____. Spy in the Vodka. New York: Morrow,
        1967.

1534   Thomson, June. The Long Revenge. Garden City,
        N. Y. : Doubleday, 1975.
        An anonymous letter to a retiring British in-
        telligence agent sets forth a desperate hunt for a
        threatening killer.

1535   Thorp, Duncan. Over the Wall. New York: Pinnacle
        Books, 1973. P
        Five men and a woman fight amongst themselves
        and plot a Caribbean revolution against a brutal and
        powerful dictator whose rule has been absolute for
        years.

1536   Thurburn, Rose. Wilderness Is Yours. New York:
        Morrow, 1950.
        Slade, a ruthless, self-seeking government of-
        ficial, encounters the mysterious Patkov during a
        war between two minor unnamed European nations.

1537   Tickell, Jerrard. High Water at Four. Garden City,
        N. Y. : Doubleday, 1966.
        Court-martialed and cashiered Cmdr. Millerton
        is given a berth aboard the yacht of a Greek mil-
        lionaire and is led into a tight chase involving a
        cast of international nasties.

1538   _____. The Villa Mimosa. Garden City, N. Y. :
        Doubleday, 1961.
        A wartime raid by undercover commandos is
        made on a French brothel used as a meeting place
        for German officers plotting against Hitler. Sort
        of a risqué Dirty Dozen.

1539   Tobino, Mario. The Underground. Transl. from
        Italian by Raymond Rosenthal. Garden City, N. Y. :
        Doubleday, 1966.
        The story concerns "one segment" of the Italian
        resistance movement during the war.

1540   Torr, Dominic. Diplomatic Cover. New York:
        Harcourt, 1967.
        In Paris during a diplomatic crisis, an Ameri-
        can security official and a Soviet agent duel for the
        success of their nations' maneuvering.

1541 _____. The Treason Line. New York: Stein &
        Day, 1970.
            In Geneva during a disarmament conference,
        the Red Chinese spy chief persuades his American
        counterpart to let the Reds have America's nuclear
        fail-safe missile device.

1542 Toulmin, June. Courier to Peking. New York:
        Farrar, 1972.
            Without his knowing it, the scientist-leader of
        U.S. delegation to a Peking meeting is being used
        by American Intelligence to smuggle a secret mes-
        sage to China's leaders.

1543 Tregaskis, Richard. China Bomb. New York: Wash-
        burn, 1967.
            The famed author of Guadalcanal Diary tells of
        the activities of a small group of American agents
        assigned to destroy China's first H-bomb, which the
        Reds are planning to drop on the U.S. Seventh
        Fleet off Vietnam.

1544 Trevanian. The Eiger Sanction. New York: Crown,
        1972.
            American art professor Jonathan Hemlock moon-
        lights in the employ of the Search and Sanction
        Division of the counter-assassination bureau known
        as C11. In his last mission before retirement, he
        is sent on a top-flight mountain climbing expedition
        with three other men, one being an enemy agent.

1545 _____. The Loo Sanction. New York: Crown,
        1973.
            Agent Hemlock is dragooned by British Intelli-
        gence into trying to infiltrate a vicious gang that
        specializes in sex and incriminating photos of Eng-
        lish VIP's.

1546 Trevor, Elleston. The Mandarin Cypher. By Adam
        Hall, pseud. Garden City, N.Y.: Doubleday,
        1975.
            The redoubtable agent Quiller must penetrate
        the enemy's defenses and find a VIP held some-
        where in the South China Sea.

1547 _____. The Ninth Directive. By Adam Hall,
        pseud. New York: Simon and Schuster, 1967.

Agent Quiller of "Memorandum" fame is assigned by his agency to protect a British VIP who
is scheduled to visit Bangkok.

1548   _____. The Quiller Memorandum. By Adam Hall,
pseud. New York: Simon and Schuster, 1965.
Taking a leaf from the theme of Le Carré, our
author attempts to depict realistically the mundane
existence of real-life spies. In this famous tale,
agent Quiller is assigned to ferret out the headquarters of a neo-Nazi group running amuck in
Berlin. Quiller does not care for his automaton
assignments in the big intelligence apparatus, but
carries them out anyway, knowing in this case that
the ODESSA-like group will grow stronger in the
future even if he succeeds in taking it down a few
pegs during this outing.

1549   _____. Rook's Gambit. By Adam Hall, pseud.
New York: Simon & Schuster, 1972.

1550   _____. The Shoot. Garden City, N.Y.: Doubleday, 1966.
A diverse group is present on a remote island
where a new missile is being tested.

1551   _____. The Striker Portfolio. By Adam Hall,
pseud. New York: Simon & Schuster, 1969.
Agent Quiller must learn why three dozen
supersonic Striker aircraft have all crashed, killing
their pilots and destroying any evidence of sabotage.

1552   _____. The Tango Briefing. By Adam Hall,
pseud. Garden City, N.Y.: Doubleday, 1973.
Quiller races enemy agents to find the mystery
cargo of a plane which has crashed in the Sahara--
except he does not know exactly what he is looking
for!

1553   _____. VIP. New York: Morrow, 1960.
A reporter recognizes a VIP picked up in an
official limousine at a deserted landing strip outside London and is led into a political intrigue
which threatens to loose World War III.

1554   _____. The Warsaw Document. By Adam Hall,
pseud. Garden City, N.Y.: Doubleday, 1971.

Quiller arrives in Warsaw in the midst of an
important conference and while the underground is
planning a revolt. While he seeks to contact that
unhappy group, he is shadowed by the Russians.

1555   Tucker, Wilson. The Warlock. Garden City, N.Y.:
        Doubleday, 1968.
        A story of electronic espionage in which an
American agent/radio specialist is dropped into his
native Poland to set up a secret transmitter which
will advise the U.S. of the spy satellites Russia is
orbiting.

1556   Tute, Warren. A Matter of Diplomacy. New York:
        Coward-McCann, 1970.
        The wife of a British defector comes to Athens
as the guest of a big shipping tycoon and there con-
tacts the head of her husband's former "department,"
who has been demoted over the affair.

1557   Underwood, Michael. Reward for a Defector. New
        York: St. Martin's Press, 1974.
        An East German diplomat elects to defect and
asks the aid of an old barrister friend who is al-
ready engaged defending a spy on trial.

1558   _____. The Shadow Game. Garden City, N.Y.:
        Doubleday, 1969.

1559   _____. The Unprofessional Spy. Garden City,
        N.Y.: Doubleday, 1965.
        A London barrister accepts a job to check out
a Berlin woman he had loved years before. During
his assignment, he bitterly reaches the firm conclusion that "spying is strictly for professionals."

1560   Uris, Leon. The Angry Hills. New York: Random
        House, 1955.
        While attempting to smuggle out vital espionage
papers, an American adventurer is caught in war-
torn Greece between the retreating Allies and the
advancing Germans.

1561   _____. Topaz. New York: McGraw-Hill, 1967.
        A Russian defector tells about "Topaz," a

Soviet espionage network operating inside the French
government and of the existence of Soviet missiles
in Cuba. Based on fact.

1562   Van der Post, Laurens. Flamingo Feather. New
       York: Morrow, 1955.
           Pierre de Beauvillers searches Africa for a
       friend and ends up in a Communist-inspired plot to
       make the Black natives rise against their White
       rulers.

1563   Van Greenway, Peter. Take the War to Washington.
       New York: St. Martin's Press, 1975.
           The U.S. aircraft carrier Carolina has been
       hijacked by a tough band of battle-weary veterans
       in the Far East, who shape a course for America
       and a showdown with the President's war policy.

1564   Van Oradell, John. Ragland. Cleveland: World,
       1972.
           When the CIA discovers the Chinese may be
       trying to sneak nuclear devices into America,
       President Jeffrey Ragland comes disastrously close
       to starting a war on what eventually proves to be
       misinformation.

1565   Veraldi, Gabriel. Spies of Good Intent. Transl. from
       French by Norman Denny. New York: Atheneum,
       1969.
           A secret international body of scientists sends
       out an agent who, in cooperation with French In-
       telligence, disrupts an American plan to insert in-
       struments into the heads of various people and
       thereby control whole populations.

1566   Vicas, Victor and Victor Haim. The Impromptu Im-
       poster. New York: Abelard-Schuman, 1971.
           After accidentally killing a French policeman,
       an American escapes to Israel sans passport.
       There he is blackmailed into helping ODESSA in
       their game of killing off top Jewish officials.

1567   Vonnegut, Kurt, Jr. Mother Night. New York:
       Harper, 1966.
           Awaiting trial as a war criminal, a former

U.S. counter-intelligence officer (American by birth and Nazi by reputation) commits his life story to paper.

1568   Vorhies, John R.   Pre-Empt.   Chicago: Regnery, 1967.
The captain of a U.S. submarine offers the world an ultimatum: form an international council and surrender all nuclear weapons to the wreckers or he will let loose with his eighteen Poseidon missiles.

1569   Waddell, Martin.   Otley.   New York: Stein & Day, 1966.   H
From the moment when Gerald Otley, a British thief, steals a figurine, he is drawn into a hectic series of adventures, featuring murder and espionage.

1570   _____.   Otley Forever.   New York: Stein & Day, 1968.   H
Trouble finds Otley again when he seeks to locate a nuclear device lost by the United States.

1571   _____.   Otley Pursued.   New York: Stein & Day, 1967.   H
Our hero is now a secret agent and together with his female counterpart, Grace, is sent across the Channel to look in on neo-Nazi stirrings and mysterious cults which threaten the peace.

1572   _____.   Otley Victorious.   New York: Stein & Day, 1969.   H

1573   Wade, Jonathan.   Running Sand.   New York: Random House, 1963.
The daughter of an important American journalist is kidnapped by the Russians to keep her father from printing articles which would embarrass them at an upcoming Summit meeting.

1574   Wager, Walter.   Sledgehammer.   New York: Macmillan, 1970.
An elite group of World War II trained counter-intelligence agents take over a town to stalk the

killer of an old buddy.

1575   _____. The Swap. New York: Macmillan, 1972.

1576   _____. Telefon. New York: Macmillan, 1975.
            A large number of Russian "sleepers" left
over from an anticipated but now abandoned sabotage caper are reactivated one by one on orders
from a mad Soviet defector.

1577   _____. Viper Three. New York: Macmillan,
            1971.
            Five death-row convicts seize a missile base
and threaten to trigger World War III.

1578   Wagner, Geoffrey A. A Passionate Land. New York:
            Simon and Schuster, 1953.
            In present-day Mexico, the British ambassador
is killed by a fanatical society everyone believes to
be the creature of English cement tycoon Edward
Dodds.

1579   Wahloo, Per. The Fire Engine that Disappeared.
            New York: Pantheon, 1971.
            Agent Martin Beck is involved in several weird
occurrences: a suicide leaves a note with two
words, "Martin Beck"; an incendiary device blows
the roof off an old apartment building in Stockholm;
and a local crime seems to lead off in a number of
trails to the heart of Europe.

1580   _____. The Man Who Went Up in Smoke. New
            York: Pantheon, 1969.
            Beck is ordered to Stockholm to find a hard-
drinking Swedish reporter who knows something the
intelligence boys also want to learn.

1581   Wakeman, Frederick. A Free Agent. New York:
            Simon & Schuster, 1963.
            An intelligence officer for an unnamed govern-
ment group seeks to block the Russians and Chinese
from controlling a new African country.

1582   Walker, David. C. A. B. --Intersec. By David
            Esdaile, pseud. Boston: Houghton-Mifflin, 1968.
            Approached by Intersec, a top-level powerful
secret agency, Harry Ambler is given a mission

and must decide if he can betray the person with
whom he broke out of a German POW camp years
earlier.

1583 _____. Diamonds for Danger. By David Esdaile,
pseud. New York: Harper, 1954. H
A humorous spy story of a diamond hunt in
Portugal.

1584 Wallace, Irving. The Plot. New York: Simon &
Schuster, 1967.
The four main characters attempt to refurbish
their tarnished reputations in the shadow of a Paris
disarmament conference. As they interweave, a
plot transcending their own problems and threaten-
ing the future of mankind is uncovered.

1585 Wallis, Arthur J. and Charles F. Blair. Thunder
Above. New York: Holt, 1957.
An American aviator bound for Berlin is forced
down behind the Iron Curtain, but is helped to escape by a pretty girl. Once across, alone, our
hero decides to return to rescue her.

1586 Ware, Wallace. Charka Memorial. Garden City,
N. Y. : Doubleday, 1955.
The representative of a Central European government to Washington is summoned home to what
he knows is certain doom.

1587 Waugh, Alec. The Mule on the Minaret. New York:
Farrar, Straus & Giroux, 1966.
During World War II, Professor Noel Raid is
assigned an espionage mission which takes him to
Beirut and Baghdad for British Intelligence. Twenty
years later, he relives the job and recalls the old
Arab proverb: "a man who takes his mule to the
top of a minaret must bring it down himself."

1588 _____. A Spy in the Family. New York: Farrar,
1970.

1589 Wayland, Patrick. Double Defector. Garden City,
N. Y. : Doubleday, 1965.
Counterstroke agent Lloyd Nicolson searches
for an old friend and fellow agent who has defected
to the Russians.

1590   _____. Counterstroke. Garden City, N. Y. :
        Doubleday, 1964.
        Another Agent Nicolson tale.

1591   _____. The Waiting Game. Garden City, N. Y. :
        Doubleday, 1965.
        Following the disappearance of a beautiful
        Soviet ballerina at Kennedy airport, Nicolson tails
        his leads from Vermont to Chicago.

1592   Weeks, William R. Knock and Wait Awhile. Boston:
        Houghton-Mifflin, 1957.
        An American agent is sent to stop a girl re-
        porter from visiting the Soviet Union.

1593   Weil, Barry. Dossier IX. Indianapolis: Bobbs-
        Merrill, 1969.
        Asher, the "McCloud" of the Israeli Intelligence
        service, is on a year's training service with the
        British. The mission highlighted is his effort, with
        British and French help, to capture a turncoat
        British agent working for the Russians.

1594   Weismiller, Edward. The Serpent Sleeping. New
        York: Putnam, 1963.
        In Cherbourg just after its capture by the
        Allies, a French girl is arrested as a Nazi spy
        and wrongly prosecuted. An American private be-
        lieves her innocent and works to prove that in the
        face of stern opposition from a superior.

        Welcome, John, pseud. see Brennan, John

1595   West, Elliot. Man Running. New York: Random
        House, 1959.

1596   _____. The Night Is a Time for Listening. New
        York: Random House, 1966.
        Daross would strike a bargain with Satan him-
        self for the privilege of killing the SS agent who
        had tortured his wife to death.

1597   _____. These Lonely Victories. New York: Put-
        nam, 1972.
        East German defector Adele Webber is due to
        be exchanged for a much-needed American spy.
        U. S. Intelligence agent Brian Colman doubts the

the wisdom of the deal--so he runs off with Adele!

1598   West, Morris L. Harlequin. New York: Morrow,
        1974.
            Sophisticated computers program human beings
        to acts of assassination, kidnapping, and revolution.

1599   _____. The Salamander. New York: Morrow,
        1973.
            An Italian Colonel, seeking to preserve his life
        and find out who killed a general plotting against
        the government, has one clue: a card with a
        crowned salamander code-name signifying survival.

1600   _____. The Shoes of the Fisherman. New York:
        Morrow, 1963.
            A newly elected Pope, who spent years as a
        political prisoner in the Ukraine, has the support
        of the Russians and the Americans as he uses the
        Church's resources to feed a warlike but starving
        Asian land remarkably like China.

1601   _____. The Tower of Babel. New York: Morrow,
        1968.
            The lives of a number of Jews in Israel just
        before the Six Day War of 1967. One of those
        placed under the microscope is Jakov Baratz,
        Director of Israeli Intelligence.

1602   Westheimer, David. Lighter than a Feather. Boston:
        Little, Brown, 1971.
            What would have happened if the U.S. Joint
        Chiefs of Staff had not permitted the A-bomb to be
        dropped on Hiroshima, but instead ordered up an
        invasion known as "Operation Olympic?"

1603   Weverka, Robert. One Minute to Eternity. New
        York: Morrow, 1969.
            A Pentagon agent is sent to Mexico to find
        Cuban explosive expert.

1604   Wheeler, Keith. The Last Mayday. Garden City,
        N.Y.: Doubleday, 1969.
            When the ex-First Secretary of the Communist
        Party decides to defect, the Allies send a submarine
        to pick him up; then the Soviet Navy moves in for
        the kill.

1605   Wheeler, Paul.   And the Bullets Were Made of Lead.
       Garden City, N.Y.:   Doubleday, 1969.
            A free lance writer is in Paris attempting to
       prevent a political assassination and clear up the
       tragedy of an old friend.

1606   White, Alan.   The Long Drop.   New York: Harcourt,
       1970.
            Commando Group 404 is trained for a near-
       suicidal secret wartime operation in Belgium.

1607   _____.   The Long Fuse.   New York: Harcourt,
       1974.
            In "Operation Rundfunk," Captain Colson and
       his British Commandos jump into France, establish
       contact with the Resistance, and capture a German
       radio station for use in broadcasting Allied propa-
       ganda.

1608   _____.   The Long Midnight.   New York: Harcourt,
       1974.
            Colson and his sergeant land in German-occupied
       Norway with the twin missions of killing a quisling
       and destroying a titanium mine worked by starving
       Lithuanian prisoners.
            Two others are:

1609   _____.   Long Night's Walk.   New York: Harcourt,
       1969.

1610   _____.   Long Watch.   New York: Harcourt, 1971.

1611   White, Jon M.   The Garden Game.   Indianapolis:
       Bobbs-Merrill, 1974.
            Sent to jail for "security reasons," Intelligence
       Chief Colonel Richman is released but can find no
       sign of his old team.

1612   White, Lionel.   The House on K Street.   New York:
       Dutton, 1965.
            The scene of a plot by the Sons of Columbia to
       get the next world war over with while the U.S. is
       still strong enough to win it.

       Whittington, Henry, author see Holly, J. Hunter

1613   Willcox, Harry.   Big Water.   By Mark Derby, pseud.
       New York: Viking, 1953.

Communist agents cross swords with a former
British war hero in this post-war account of espionage and pursuit set in Singapore and Borneo.

1614 _____. Sun in the Hunter's Eye. By Mark Derby,
pseud. New York: Viking, 1958.
The trail of a cousin leads from London to
Malaya and danger.

1615 _____. Woman Hunt. By Mark Derby, pseud.
New York: Viking, 1960.
A British agent assigned to Southeast Asia is
ordered to investigate a college suspected of being
a cover for Communist activities. Other tales by
this author are:

1616 _____. Afraid of the Dart. By Mark Derby, pseud.
New York: Viking, 1952.

1617 _____. Bad Step. By Mark Derby, pseud. New
York: Viking, 1954.

1618 _____. Element of Risk. By Mark Derby, pseud.
New York: Viking, 1952.

1619 _____. Five Nights in Singapore. By Mark Derby,
pseud. New York: Viking, 1961.

1620 _____. Sunlit Ambush. By Mark Derby, pseud.
New York: Viking, 1955.

1621 Wilkinson, Burke. Last Clear Chance. Boston:
Little, Brown, 1954. *
This spy story set in Washington, D.C., re-
volves around many of the headlines of the Cold
War and McCarthy Era.

1622 _____. Night of the Short Knives. New York:
Scribner's, 1965.
A tale of adventure and espionage set in
S.H.A.P.E., the present-day Supreme Headquarters
Allied Powers Europe.

1623 Williams, Alan. The Beria Papers. New York:
Simon & Schuster, 1973.
A pair of American writers forge and publish
the supposed diaries of Soviet secret police chief
Lavrenti Beria.

1624 _____. The Tale of the Lazy Dog. New York:
Simon & Schuster, 1971. *

Could Murray Wilde's rag-tag gang of adventurers succeed in stealing $1 million out from under
the nose of the American Army?

1625   Williams, Eric.   The Borders of Barbarism.   New
York: Coward-McCann, 1963.
The Startes return to the Balkans once more
to engage in amateur espionage.   This is the sequel
to Dragoman Pass, below.

1626   _____.   Dragoman Pass.   New York: Coward-
McCann, 1960.
Writer Roger Starte and his wife Kaţe are touring
the Balkans by jeep and become involved in smuggling
an English anthropologist and former Communist out
of Rumania.

1627   Willis, Anthony A.   Room at the Hotel Ambre.   By
Anthony Armstrong, pseud.   Garden City, N. Y. :
Doubleday, 1956.
Jane, English, wants to look at French life and
checks into a Paris hotel.   By coincidence, she has
picked the very establishment used by a Communist spy
ring as its headquarters.   Noticing that something is
amiss, she spills her thoughts to another young Britisher she meets, who just happens to be an intelligence
officer there to look into the situation.

1628   Willis, Ted.   Westminster One.   New York: Putnam, 1975.
When the abduction of the Prime Minister plunges
Britain into social and political turmoil, British Intelligence and Scotland Yard are left to ferret out
the truth of the affair.

1629   Wilson, Mitchell A.   Stalk the Hunter.   New York:
Simon & Schuster, 1953.   *
Harassed in Manhatten by Nazi agents, a young
Czech girl is saved by an American chemist.

1630   Winston, Peter.   The ABC Affair.   New York: Award,
1967.   P
Here is another of those Nick Carter-type action-
espionage series which have appeared so abundantly
in an exclusively paperback format.   In this one our
hero-narrator works for a secret organization known
as "The Adjusters" and battles a ruthless warmonger
whose plans can destroy the world.

1631   _____. Assignment to Bahrein. New York: Award,
            1968. P
                 Adjusters' agent Peter Winston foils assassina-
            tion attempts and torture, Arab style, in a powder-
            keg sheikdom.

1632   _____. Doomsday Vendetta. New York: Award,
            1969. P
                 Winston must seduce a beautiful enemy spy--
            whose lovers always end up dead!

1633   _____. The Glass Cipher. New York: Award,
            1968. P
                 An ominous message arrives from a scientist
            in China warning of a monstrous new weapon that
            could destroy America's missiles; Winston hunts
            for the mysterious Red spy who has already mur-
            dered the key man in the betrayal of this weird,
            kill-America plot.

1634   _____. The Temple at Ilumquh. New York:
            Award, 1969. P

1635   Winterton, Paul. The Ascent of D-13. By Andrew
            Garve, pseud. New York: Harper, 1969.
                 A Russian agent attempts to hijack a plane
            carrying a new detection device, but succeeds only
            in cracking it up on the summit of D-13, a nasty
            peak on the Soviet-Turkish border. The Soviets
            send a recovery team as do the British, led by one
            of their best mountain climbers.

1636   _____. The Ashes of Loda. By Andrew Garve,
            pseud. New York: Harper, 1965.
                 A correspondent begins asking why the Soviets
            accused his girlfriend's father of war crimes.

1637   _____. A Hero for Leanda. By Andrew Garve,
            pseud. New York: Harper, 1959.
                 Mike is offered a deal by millionaire Metavas:
            sail to Heureuse, a thousand miles from any land,
            and rescue Kastella, the political leader of Spyros,
            who is being held by the British.

1638   Winton, John. The Fighting Temeraire. New York:
            Coward-McCann, 1971. *
                 In the silent war between Russia and the West,

a nuclear submarine enters the Black Sea on a secret mission which becomes an international incident.

1639   Wittman, George. A Matter of Intelligence. New
York: Macmillan, 1975.
A KGB agent posing as a loyal American fum-
bles his mission to steal US missile secrets.

1640   Wolfe, Michael. Man on a String. New York: Harper, 1973.
The sinister Colonel Xe of the ARVN lures an
American officer into an ingenious scheme to retrieve a huge U.S. payroll "lost" years before in
the mountains north of Saigon.

1641   Wolk, George. The Leopard Contract. New York:
Random House, 1969.
An American operative works to liquidate an
enemy spy while posing as bodyguard to an American scientist.

1642   Wood, James. The Sealer. New York: Vanguard,
1961.
Jim Fraser, a Scotch shepherd and fisherman,
relates his mission to ferret out a secret Nazi
raider in the waters of Tierra del Fuego. Other
nautical-espionage tales featuring Jim Fraser include:

1643   _____. Fire Rock. New York: Vanguard, 1966.

1644   _____. Friday Run. New York: Vanguard, 1970.

1645   _____. Lisa Bastian. New York: Vanguard, 1961.

1646   _____. Northern Missions. New York: Vanguard,
1954.

1647   _____. Rain Islands. New York: Vanguard, 1957.

1648   _____. Three Blind Mice. New York: Vanguard,
1971.

1649   Woodhouse, Martin. Blue Bone. New York: Coward-
McCann, 1973.
A Giles Yeoman, British hero, story.

1650   _____. Bush Boy. New York: Coward-McCann,
1969.
Someone has tampered with an automatic

seismograph and Yeoman, sent to locate it, uncovers a dangerous laser crystal which certain
Albanian agents want.

1651 _____. Mama Doll. New York: Coward-McCann,
1972.
Yeoman recovers from surgery filled with the
fires of vengeance.

1652 _____. Tree Frog. New York: Coward-McCann,
1966.
Yeoman is doped and whisked off to a Polish
hideout in the Tyrolean Alps where his captors tor-
ture him for data concerning a new pilotless reconnaissance plane nicknamed "Tree Frog."

1653 Wren, M. K. Curiosity Didn't Kill the Cat. Garden
City, N.Y.: Doubleday, 1973.
When a Navy captain is found dead in Oregon,
the grieving wife calls in a secret agent to find out
"who done it." As much a detective story as a
spy caper.

1654 Wuorio, Eva-Lis. The Woman with the Portugese
Basket. New York: Holt, 1965. *
In the manner of Helen MacInnes, this is a
suspense tale of espionage in which Kari, a Finnish-
American artist, and Adelaide, a middle-aged art
teacher on sabbatical from Toronto, follow separate
paths across Europe to meet in present-day Vienna.

1655 _____. Z for Zaborra. New York: Holt, 1966.
Toria Walden, an ex-agent, carries on a deadly
masquerade for British Intelligence in a hospital
where a courier from a neo-Nazi organization is
supposed to deliver information dangerous to the
whole world.

1656 Wylie, Philip. Smuggled Atom Bomb. Garden City,
N.Y.: Doubleday, 1965.
Some nasties have come into the possession of
an A-bomb and plan to use it for blackmail purposes.

1657 _____. The Spy Who Spoke Porpoise. Garden
City, N.Y.: Doubleday, 1970.
A retired American intelligence agent is

secretly commissioned by the President to sneak
information out of the CIA and with the help of a
porpoise, halt a Communist plot against Hawaii.

1658 Wynd, Oswald. The Bitter Tea. By Gavin Black,
      pseud. New York: Harper, 1972.
      Malaysian businessman Paul Harris becomes
      involved in the kidnapping of a high Chinese official.

1659 _____. The Cold Jungle. By Gavin Black, pseud.
      New York: Harper, 1969.
      Harris returns to England from Malaysia to
      have a ship built for his company by an old friend.
      Pressure is put on him, the friend is murdered,
      and our hero is threatened in various ways by an
      unknown power for apparently unknown reasons.

1660 _____. Death, the Red Flower. By Gavin Black,
      pseud. New York: Harcourt, 1961.
      The captain of a British freighter is the un-
      knowing dupe in a Communist plot to start World
      War III.

1661 _____. A Dragon for Christmas. By Gavin Black,
      pseud. New York: Harper, 1963.
      Harris gets mixed up in foreign intrigue while
      attempting to peddle his wares in Peking.

1662 _____. The Eyes Around Me. By Gavin Black,
      pseud. New York: Harper, 1964.
      A murder-intrigue involving a lovely girl found
      dead in her Hong Kong bed and a Scot wrongly
      singled out as chief suspect in an unhappy scheme.

1663 _____. The Golden Cockatrice. By Gavin Black,
      pseud. New York: Harper, 1975.
      Harris is caught in the middle of a Chinese-
      Russian shipping rivalry.

1664 _____. Sumatra Seven Zero. New York: Har-
      court, 1968.
      A retired British Intelligence officer named
      McFay is recalled to help his old agency find the
      missing daughter of a murdered Burmese ruby mine
      owner.

1665 _____. A Time of Pirates. By Gavin Black,

pseud. New York: Harper, 1971.
Harris is involved with a group of murderous
modern-day buccaneers operating off the coasts of
Malaysia.

1666 _____. Walk Softly, Men Praying. New York:
Harcourt, 1967.
Ian Douglas meets CIA agent Calcotl, who needs
information about some strange exports from Japan
to China.

1667 Yates, Brock. Dead in the Water. New York:
Farrar, 1975.
Terrorists plot to kidnap the Canadian Prime
Minister.

1668 Yates, Margaret. Murder by the Yard. New York:
Macmillan, 1942. *
A girl agent follows a Japanese operative in
Honolulu in the days just before Pearl Harbor.

1669 Yerby, Frank. The Voyage Unplanned. New York:
Dial Press, 1974.
Searching for a comrade-in-arms twenty years
after the end of the war, a French Resistance
fighter is drawn into a bloody angle of the Arab-
Israeli conflict.

York, Andrew, pseud. see Nicole, Christopher

1670 Young, Edward P. The Fifth Passenger. New York:
Harper, 1963.
A London solicitor is on the spot when a defecting naval officer, who saved his life years before, seeks his aid. Librarian friends reading this
thriller will be pleased to note that the great chase
scene takes place through the stacks of the London
Public Library.

1671 Zarubica, Mladin. Scutari. New York: Farrar, 1968.
American businessman Urosh Gore becomes an
unwitting cog in a plan which sends him to Albania
to penetrate a Red Chinese missile base.

1672   . The Year of the Rat. New York: Harcourt, 1965. *
A hunting guide in the Alps tells of a hoax in
which Allied Intelligence substituted their own agent
for his double, a German courier general, to get
false plans for "Operation Overlord" (D-Day) into
German hands.

1673 Zeno. Grab. New York: Stein & Day, 1971.
A mercenary accepts a job to "escort" a certain Arab out of Libya.

1674 Zerwick, Chloë and Harrison Brown. The Cassiopeia
Affair. Garden City, N.Y.: Doubleday, 1968. *
Dr. Max Gaby, a Presidential assistant, receives a special signal from Cassiopeia and dies of
a stroke. Later, in China, another scientist receives a similar message. This is a different type
of thriller, a cross between intrigue, espionage,
and science fiction.

1675 Zilinsky, Ursula. Before the Glory Ended. Philadelphia: Lippincott, 1967.
The decline of the aristocracy and the changes
which rocked Europe between 1919 and 1957 are
viewed through the eyes of two men, a French spy
and a Hungarian agent.

TITLE INDEX

203